Sanger Brown

Sex Worship

An exposition of the phallic origin of religion

Sanger Brown

Sex Worship
An exposition of the phallic origin of religion

ISBN/EAN: 9783337036744

Printed in Europe, USA, Canada, Australia, Japan

Cover: Foto ©Lupo / pixelio.de

More available books at **www.hansebooks.com**

SEX WORSHIP:

AN EXPOSITION OF THE PHALLIC
ORIGIN OF RELIGION.

BY
CLIFFORD HOWARD.

Washington, D. C.
PUBLISHED BY THE AUTHOR.
1897.

COPYRIGHT
BY CLIFFORD HOWARD,
1897.

CONTENTS.

Introduction		7
Chapter I.	The Basis of Religion	13
Chapter II.	The Male Principle	26
Chapter III.	The Phallus	42
Chapter IV.	Phallic Emblems	61
Chapter V.	Sexual Sacrifices	77
Chapter VI.	The Female Principle	90
Chapter VII.	Feminine Emblems	102
Chapter VIII.	The Serpent and the Cross	123
Chapter IX.	The Divine Act	138
Chapter X.	Regeneration	153

INTRODUCTION.

No subject is of greater importance and significance in the history of the human race than that of sex worship, the adoration of the generative organs and their functions as symbols of the procreative powers of nature. It was the universal primitive religion of the world and has left its indelible impress upon our ideas, our language and our institutions. It constitutes the basis of all religious systems and the origin of our most sacred symbols and many of our most familiar customs; in a word, it is the foundation of religious thought and conduct.

Phallic (sex) worship was not confined to any one race nor to any particular age in the history of the world, but was the religion of all nations at all times. It was the worship inspired by the phenomena of nature in her great mystery of life, and while its resultant mythologies and attendant ceremonials were carried and adapted from one nation to another, it had numerous independent originations; for the human mind, as a whole, is always affected in the same way under similar conditions, and the wondrous phenomenon of procreation has ever aroused in primitive man a deep and religious reverence for the animating powers of life.

While the highest development of phallicism was reached by the ancient Egyptians, Hindoos, Assyrians, Greeks and Romans, whose records and remains abound in evidence of the phallic basis of their elaborate mythologies and religious celebrations, the existence of this early form of religion is to be found in every part of the globe inhabited by man. Babylon, Persia, Hindustan, Ceylon, China, Japan, Burmah, Java, Arabia, Syria, Asia Minor, Egypt, Ethiopia, Europe, the British Isles, Mexico, Yucatan, Peru and various other parts of America—all yield abundant evidence to the same effect and point to a common origin of religious beliefs.

It must not, however, be imagined that phallic worship is a religion belonging entirely to the past ages. It is common among primitive races in all parts of the world to-day ; and in India, where this form of religion has existed uninterruptedly since its foundation, thousands of years ago, there are at the present time upwards of one hundred million true phallic-worshippers. Among the Zuñi and other North American tribes phallicism enters into a number of their religious ceremonies, while the natives of many of the Pacific islands and certain parts of Africa are most ardent devotees in the worship of the procreative functions, and exhibit their religion in the realistic and unequivocal manner of primeval naturalness.

Phallicism is a well-nigh limitless subject, entering as it does into every stage in the evolution of human thought and conduct. A thorough and exhaustive treatment of the subject would require many large volumes, and the present work is designed simply as an outline, for the purpose of setting forth some of the principal and more salient features of sex worship, in testimony of the natural basis and common origin of religious faiths. No attempt has been made to discuss the more abstruse and subtle phases of the subject, which, although of great value and interest, could not appropriately be treated in a work of so general a character as the present one.

Up to this time the subject has been confined to a small class of scholars and investigators, whose works are exceedingly difficult to obtain, both by reason of their rarity and costliness, and, in consequence, the general reader has had little or no opportunity of acquainting himself with the revelations of this important subject. Furthermore, the majority of these works are of a technical or abstruse character, while many of them are written in other languages or contain numerous untranslated quotations from Greek, Latin, French, Italian and other foreign authors; so that notwithstanding the interest of the subject, its general mode of presentation has been such as to render it unattractive, except to the special student, even though an opportunity of studying the subject had been presented.

The present work embodies a large

amount of original research, besides that of investigators both ancient and modern, all of whose works have been carefully studied, and has for its object, in addition to its primary purpose of demonstrating the phallic origin of religious worship, a popular presentation of this important and interesting subject, in the belief that it will be received and appreciated by the thoughtful and intelligent public, for whom it is alone designed, in the spirit that its value and significance deserve.

In viewing the forms and ceremonials connected with the nature-worship of primitive civilization, it should be constantly borne in mind that they are not always to be understood in their direct and obvious sense, but are to be considered as symbolical representations of that which is pure and holy, and that the teachings and rites of sex worship were as sacred and dear to the pious devotees of those early days as are the principles of our religion to us. It must be remembered that religion, in whatever form it may be manifested, always represents man's highest and purest thought;

that no one would deliberately introduce into his religious worship anything that to his mind is impure.

Therefore, however extravagant or absurd phallic worship may appear to us at this day, let us not forget that it represents a stage in the evolution of the human mind; that it was man's religion at the dawn of civilization, and that the grandest theologies of to-day are the outcome of this primitive worship; that it constitutes the basis of all that is sacred, holy and beautiful.

CHAPTER I.

THE BASIS OF RELIGION.

Of all the phenomena of nature there is none that has always so strongly excited the wonder and reverence of mankind as that of procreation—the transmission of life from one generation to another. At all times and on all hands we behold nature engaged in her ceaseless work of reproduction, and yet the mystery of that wondrous creative power, which causes the plant to spring from the tiny seed and brings the child—a new being—into the world, is to-day as deep and inspiring as it was to the mind of man in the early dawn of the world's history.

One of the first problems of human thought is that regarding creation. Where do we come from? How is life produced? Who brings the new beings into the world? are the natural and innocent questions that perplex the mind of every child; and when, from a sense of modesty, we evade an explanation of the physical features of reproduction by telling the little one that God is the author of all life, it is simply an admission on our part that we regard the creative power as emanating from a source beyond ourselves, and that we are, therefore, really no wiser than the child ; for our acquaintance with the generative functions and our knowledge of the part they play in the phenomenon of procreation only add to the mystery, and render the secret of life all the more wonderful and incomprehensible.

In fact, it is the means by which generation is accomplished that appeals to man with greater force and impressiveness, and exerts a more potent influence upon his ideas and conduct, than aught else in the world. That affinity which draws the two sexes together for the purpose of uniting in the production of a new being ; that overmastering, universal impulse—the sexual instinct—is the most powerful factor in all that pertains to the human race, and has ever been the object of man's reverence and worship.

In this day and age, when matters pertaining to the sexes are generally avoided, and we are taught that the sexual appetite is an animal craving that should be subdued and concealed as unworthy of man's superior nature, it is not surprising that the great majority of persons are blind to the vast importance and significance of the sexual nature in its relation to the affairs of the world, and that they fail to realize that not only is it the cause of our individual existence, but that it is the foundation of all society and the well-spring of human life and happiness.

It is not our purpose here to enter upon a discussion of the physiological features of the subject, showing the intimate and unavoidable relationship existing between the mind and the sexual instinct ; but suffice it to say, that were man deprived of this instinct it would not only result in the extermination of the race (for procreation would be impossible in the absence of this animating desire), but all ambition, endeavor and affection, all poetry, art and religion—in short, all the emotions and achievements inspired by what we term " love," would cease, and the world would become cold and passionless, destitute of sentiment or aspiration, devoid of any incentive to progress or energy, while the intricate and reciprocal machinery of human society, robbed of its motive force, would come to a stop and crumble away in hopeless disorganization.

It is universally admitted that love is the animating spirit of the world ; and what is love but a manifestation of the sexual instinct ? The civilized man, who woos the object of his affection through the medium of inspired poetry and other sentimental graces, who reveals the longings of his heart in language and conduct at once pure, exalted and tender, and who instinctively shrinks from the suggestion of any sensuality in his feelings, is nevertheless actuated by precisely the same motive as that which governs the savage in his brutal and uncouth demonstration of desire toward one of the opposite sex. Each is but giving expression, in accordance with his individual nature and social conditions, to the same feeling, the same impulse. In the one case we recognize it as love ; in the other, as sensuality ; yet both spring from the same source ; both are animated by the same instinct.

Whatever reluctance there may be in admitting this physical truth, is due to the unfortunate fact that we have been taught to regard the generative nature as confined wholly within the narrow limits of its purely sensual manifestations, as exhibited in lust and mere animal gratification ; and, consequently, we fail to appreciate it in its higher, nobler and all-pervading form of love. But viewing it in its broad and true aspect, untrammeled by arbitrary definitions, we are forced to admit its vital importance as the supreme factor in the life and welfare of the human race.

Love, as an abstract power, is ever glorified and idealized, because we see in it the source, the inspiration, of all beauty, morality and sublimity ; the incentive to deeds of the highest and noblest character ; the elevating and controlling spirit of man's life. Every poet, every artist, every composer, all who are gifted with the power of most truly expressing the loftiest emotions and feelings of mankind have found their inspiration in the inexhaustible theme of love; and no language, no expression, has ever been deemed too exalted, too far-reaching, for the portrayal of this universal and omnipotent passion.

In our idealization of love it soars beyond the bounds of earthly limitations, and we hesitate not to ascribe to it a divine character and embrace it in the most sacred and exalted sphere of man's intellectual domain —religion. Nay, do we not raise it to the highest point capable of attainment by the human mind, when we reverently exclaim, " God is love ! "—when we bow down and worship it as the divine essence, the supreme power ?

It is not within the province of this work to attempt a complete analysis of love, or sexuality, in its complex relation to these higher and more subtle phases of human thought and conduct; but enough has been said to indicate that the animating spirit of the human mind—the underlying principle of its lofty and holy emotions—is the spiritualizing power of love ; that this impulse lies at the foundation of all thought and action, and finds its grandest and most exalted expression in religion.

Love is both the foundation and the pinnacle of religion ; the beginning and the end of human thought and aspiration. Religious emotion springs from the animating power of love, and through the emotion thus aroused we deify and worship the inspirational source of our spiritual longings. In every sense, both physical and spiritual, both material and ideal, love is the animating, creative force of the world ; the divine immanence of the universe ; the actuating source of life and the indwelling spirit of the soul ; the beginning and end of all that is.

It is not intended, however, that the proof of the basis of religious worship shall alone rest upon a physiological analysis, however complete or demonstrative, but that the records of human history shall bear witness to the fact that theology has sprung from the animating impulse of life, and that it has for its primary and universal object the worship of its inspiring cause; the worship of the mystery of life, of creation and reproduction; the worship of the omnipotent creative power.

When the ambassador from the French court presented to the Buddhist king of Siam the request of Louis XIV that he would embrace Christianity, he replied: "It is strange that the king of France should interest himself so much in a matter which concerns only God, whilst He whom it does concern seems to have left it wholly to our discretion. Had it been agreeable to the Creator that all nations should have the same form of worship, would it not have been as easy for him in his omnipotence to have created all men with the same sentiments and dispositions and to have inspired them with the same notions of the True Religion, as to endow them with such different tempers and inclinations? Ought we not rather to believe that the true God has as much pleasure in being honored by a variety of forms and ceremonies as in being praised and glorified by a number of different creatures?"

"Even they who worship other gods," says Krishna, the incarnate deity, in an ancient Hindu poem, "worship me although they know it not."

These expressions embody the teachings of the higher philosophy of the Buddhist and Hindu religions, which recognize the true source and motive of all religious faiths, and the glorious universality of "the true religion." To them there is but one religion; one supreme, everlasting truth; the so-called different religions of the world being but different modes of manifesting and expressing this eternal truth.

It is apparent to everyone who has had an opportunity of studying the subject, that all religious faiths have had a common origin, and that however much they may differ in their teachings and institutions, they but represent different methods of worshipping one and the same object. Brahma, Jehovah, God, Allah and hundreds of others are simply different names for the same deity, as viewed from different standpoints; and this deity, this universal object of adoration, is the supreme creative power.

No two individuals, however closely related by birth and circumstances, ever view the same object in exactly the same light. Much less, therefore, can we expect widely separated nations, living under entirely different conditions, to resemble one another in their views and customs and to construct similar systems of morality and church government. Each builds its social and theological structure in accordance with its ideas and needs; each constructs a form of religion suitable to its conditions mental and physical. Every being, every race, every age, has a religion in conformity with its individual status and necessities. The savage no more comprehends our abstract, impersonal conception of the Almighty, than can we understand his abject reverence for a hideous wooden idol; yet both the savage and ourselves are worshiping identically the same object and are actuated by the same motive.

These facts become all the more apparent when we note how great is the diversity of thought and conduct among people of the same community and of the same religious faith. Do we not see Christianity broken up into a multitude of sects and denominations, each observing the same religion in a different manner ? When we trace the development of Christian civilization back through the past centuries, we find that religious notions and customs have been constantly changing, and that what we call Christianity has embraced every conceivable variety of thought and conduct ; that it has served as the authority for practices and institutions which at another time have been condemned and forbidden by the same authority. The Inquisition flourished in its name, the glorious Crusades were carried on under its banners ; we have seen it casting gloom and misery upon the earth, and we have beheld it bringing joy and liberty to the world. But, despite these marvelous changes and contradictions, who will say that Christianity itself has changed; that the foundation on which it rests has been shaken ? The fundamental doctrines have remained unaltered ; they have simply been modified and adapted to the various stages in the evolution of human thought, now appearing in one form and now in another, concordantly with the moral and intellectual development of the race.

So, also, do we find that many of the main features of Christianity are simply modifications or adaptations of those existing in older forms of religion; that long prior to the time of Christ mankind worshiped a Creator in the form of a Triune God; that the Hindoos, Assyrians, Babylonians and other ancient people each had their supreme creative Trinity; that the belief in a Saviour, a son of God, who was born of a virgin, died for the salvation of man and rose again after death, dates back centuries and thousands of years before the Christian era, as we see in the ancient faiths of Egypt, China and India.

In short, we find that the fundamental religious beliefs of the world have remained unchanged from time immemorial, however diversified and varied have been their superincumbent theologies, and that beneath the outward and ceremonial differences of the various faiths of mankind, throughout all the world and throughout all the ages of human history, there are to be found the same legends and the same doctrines, all pointing to a common origin, to a universal foundation—the worship of nature in its great mystery of life and procreation.

CHAPTER II.

THE MALE PRINCIPLE.

As was stated in the preceding chapter, the phenomenon of procreation has ever been the source of deepest interest, curiosity and reverence, and we may readily imagine how strangely and forcibly it must have impressed itself upon the mind of man in those early days of his social development, when he was more directly dependent upon nature than he is now and when the necessities of his condition rendered him keenly observant of all phenomena. In the infancy of man's mentality the manifestations of nature were unintelligible, but with that instinct which is still inherent in the human race, he struggled with his finite mind to grasp the infinite, and in his vain endeavor to comprehend the forces and wonders of the universe he clothed them with the imagery of his untutored mind, and they became to him living entities like himself ; the personifications of his emotions and desires; the representations of superior beings, upon whom he was dependent for his existence and happiness.

Naturally, he learned to regard most highly that which not only afforded him the greatest pleasure and the greatest good, but which appeared to him as the most powerful and the most incomprehensible, and thus it was that he came to look upon the generative power as superior to aught else. The creative act was his incomparably greatest pleasure and produced the most wonderful and most-prized result—a new being like himself. Surely, within the range of his observation and experience there was nothing in nature at once so mysterious, so potent, so awe-inspiring; so overpowering in its manifestations, so inexplicably marvelous in its results; silent and invisible in its operations; omnipotent and supreme in its powers and capabilities.

Man's first impulse is to suppose that the immediately preceding act is the cause of the immediately succeeding result, and it was therefore only natural that at first man should have regarded his virile member as the direct and sole cause of both his pleasure and of his offspring; it was through it that the greatest of all things in nature was accomplished,—a wonderful and potent instrument, endowed apparently with independent life and activity and possessed of a power transcending all others in greatness and mystery.

Hence it was that he exalted and worshiped the male organ,—the phallus; worshiped it not only as the creator of human life, but as the personification of the world's creator, or the symbol of the procreative diety; for, in common with all the other manifestations of nature, the generative power was deified; it was ascribed to a divine personality, an omnipotent, masculine god, who was the Creator, the Father, of all things, and hence the supreme deity. His power was almighty; it was he who controlled life and procreation, and the phallus was his living and sacred emblem, as the divine instrumentality through which he accomplished his glorious works.

It required a long time for mankind to reach that stage in which the mind was capable of formulating and grasping abstract notions ; of disassociating attributes and feelings from the objects in which they are manifested ; of comprehending a power or an emotion without some visible and suggestive symbol ; and so it was that the phallus became the divine object of veneration, as the symbol, if not the real person, of the Author of Life.

When we consider the supreme importance attached to the begetting of children, in ancient times, we can more readily comprehend the veneration felt for the organ of generation as their creator ; as the divine instrumentality through which a man's and woman's life duty was fulfilled. Barrenness was not only an affliction, but a curse. To be childless was to a woman worse than death. It was the supreme religious duty of every woman to bear children and perpetuate the seed of mankind, and it was at the same time the highest ambition of every man to beget sons and daughters. Of this we have ample evidence in the Scriptures and other ancient records.

We are told, for example, how earnestly

Abraham and Sarah longed for a child and that in their extremity "Sarai said unto Abram, Behold now the Lord hath restrained me from bearing; I pray thee go in unto my maid; it may be that I may obtain children by her. And Abram hearkened to the voice of Sarai."

So, also, we read of the despair of Rachel at her barrenness—" Give me children, or else I die!" and she, too, as a last resort, gave her maid to her husband, in order to thus in a measure palliate her affliction. And, again, we learn of the misery endured by Hannah, "because the Lord had shut up her womb. And she was in bitterness of soul, and prayed unto the Lord, and wept sore."

To die a virgin, as Jephthah's daughter was obliged to do,—to die without having borne children,—was an awful punishment and curse in the eyes of the ancient world. Rather than submit to the possibility of such a fate women would resort to deceit, treachery and crime, as justifiable under the circumstances; as we see in the case of Tamar, who deceived her father-in-law, and in the story of Lot's daughters, who committed incest with their father, because of their secluded abode in a cave in the mountain, "where no man could come in unto them." In short, the begetting of children was the highest and holiest aim in life, the sole purpose of human existence; an ancient belief which is so abundantly demonstrated in the Old Testament, and so well known, as scarcely to require particular mention here.

Naturally, the woman as well as the man looked to the Creator as the supreme source of her happiness and comfort. Through him alone could she obtain the greatest of all blessings and the accomplishment of life's purpose; and it was to him, therefore, that the woman prayed for children, even as the woman of to-day prays to God for a similar blessing. But to the woman of the past the Creator was not an abstract, impersonal, undefinable being. To her he was a substantial actuality, existing for a specific and well-defined purpose; closely and definitely associated with the object of her prayers. He was directly and personally concerned in the act of generation, the sole and supreme purpose for which he had brought mankind into the world. It was the Creator himself who came to her, through the medium of the man. The phallus was his divine personality, his actual presence in material form and potent activity.

That this was the idea entertained of the Creator in ancient times is shown by the biblical expression, "The Lord came in unto her;" meaning that the woman had conceived; that the Creator had manifested himself unto her through his divine personality in the shape of the male organ of generation; as we see, for example, in the 21st chapter of Genesis, relating to the conception and birth of Isaac: "And the Lord visited Sarah as he had said, and the Lord did unto Sarah as he had spoken."

It is evident, therefore, that the idea of the Creator was very closely associated with what his name specifically signifies. The phallus was his most sacred emblem or representative, and, according to the Old Testament, it is clearly shown that the God of the Hebrews so regarded it himself; for the Lord ordained that it should be specially marked and should thus constitute the sacred token of the contract between himself and his chosen people, and to this day the rite of circumcision is practised by the Jews in accordance with this command, which Jehovah gave to Abraham, the father of the Israelites, nineteen hundred years before Christ : " And God said unto Abraham, This is my covenant, which ye shall keep between me and you and thy seed after thee ; every man child among you shall be circumcised. And ye shall circumcise the flesh of your foreskin ; and it shall be a token of the covenant betwixt me and you. He that is born in thy house and he that is bought with thy money must needs be circumcised ; and my covenant shall be in your flesh for an everlasting covenant."

That the virile member was considered as specially sacred to the Creator, either as his symbol or as the instrument by which his divine power was fulfilled, is universally evidenced in all the ancient faiths and customs. In addition to the rite of circumcision just mentioned, the Old Testament affords numerous examples of the holiness attached to this symbol. It was a common custom among the Hebrews, when taking a solemn oath, to lay the hands upon the generative organ of the person to whom the vow or promise was given. This was as solemn and devout a procedure as is the present method of kissing the Bible or holding up the right hand, and was indicative of the same meaning—that of calling upon God to witness the truth and sincerity of the oath.

This custom is referred to in the 24th chapter of Genesis, where we are told that "Abraham said unto his eldest servant, Put, I pray thee, thy hand under my thigh: and I will make thee swear by the Lord, the God of Heaven and the God of the Earth, etc.," and again, in the 47th chapter of the same book, it is recorded that when Jacob was about to die he called Joseph to him and bade him put his hand under his thigh, and promise that he would not bury him in Egypt. This practice is still to be found in certain parts of Arabia and Africa, and various customs of a like character might be cited in further evidence of the sacred relationship supposed to exist between the organ of generation and the Creator. It was through it that the Creator manifested his supreme power, and hence it was an object of reverence and worship, even as was the Creator himself.

In many instances prayers were devoutly offered to the symbol, in the belief that God was thereby being addressed, and the primitive belief in the actual presence of the Creator in the generative act is again shown by the ancient religious practice of women who submitted themselves to the embraces of the priests as the divine representatives of God. This practice was not an unusual one, and was resorted to especially by barren women, in the devout belief that by this means they secured divine intercourse with the god, or the procreative deity, and thereby rendered certain their chances for bearing children.

This custom is still practised in India, and it is not uncommon for a husband to accompany his wife to the priest and remain a reverential spectator of the act representing the union of God and the woman. In various parts of India certain days are set apart in each year for the visitation of the creative deity, on which occasions the women repair to the temples and there receive from the priests the sacred blessing that they are unable to obtain from the Creator through the medium of their husbands.

Next in importance to procreation itself, is the cause that determines the sex of the offspring. Why should a man beget a son at one time and a daughter at another? What is the reason for this sexual difference? This is the question we are vainly asking ourselves to-day and is the same question that bothered the minds of men in the past ages. Naturally, an explanation was looked for in some characteristic of the phallus as the responsible creator; and while this did not lead to a complete solution of the mystery, it resulted in the important discovery that the appendages of the organ play an important and necessary part in the act of creation, and the difference in their relative size and position gave rise to the theory—which is held by many at the present day,—that the right testicle is the producer of the stronger sex, while the left or smaller one is responsible for the women of the world. That this belief was generally entertained by the ancients is evidenced by the allusions to it in the early records, including the Old Testament, where fathers refer to their sons as the children of their right side.

It became evident, therefore, that the perfect creator consisted of three parts, each distinct and complete in itself, but so dependent one upon the other for the fulfillment of their office, that it was only in their unity and co-operation that they were capable of productive activity as an absolute and perfect One.

From this it is not difficult to understand how the creative deity came to be regarded as a triune being, nor should it be surprising to learn, therefore, that the worship of a trinity dates back to the dimmest and most remote past. The Assyrians, one of the most ancient nations of the world, worshiped a trinity known as Asshur, Anu and

Hoa, and upon a study of the derivation of these names we find that they refer directly to the triune generative organ. Asshur represents the phallus, for the name plainly signifies "the erect one," "the upright member." The right testicle, which, as the assistant in the production of male children, was held next in rank to the phallus itself, is represented by Anu, a name derived from the word meaning *strength*, particularly manly strength or power, while Hoa, the third member of the trinity, has reference to the feminine element.

In this, as in all subsequent trinities of theology, the individuals composing it were of relative rank; three distinct entities or members, each necessary to the other, working together as one toward one end. As a whole they constituted the supreme god, the Creator, under the collective name of Bel. While the custom of giving to a trinity a name distinct from any of its component individuals is a common one in all religions, it is not generally observed, for, as a rule, the Trinity, or complete Creator, is known under the name of the first in rank,—as Asshur, the Lord of Lords.

We find, therefore, that the triune composition of the masculine creator was early recognized, and the veneration in which the complete and perfect male organ was held is most clearly shown by the fact that it was the subject of religious ordinances. Of this we find ample demonstration in the Old Testament, where, for example, in the 23d chapter of Deuteronomy, we learn that Jehovah himself ordained that " he that is wounded in the stones, or hath his privy member cut off, shall not enter the congregation of the Lord," plainly indicating the divine importance attached to the perfect condition of this symbol of the Creator.

This holy regard for the soundness and at the same time for the safety of the generative organ is perhaps more fully shown in the 25th chapter of the same book, where it is commanded by the Lord that a woman shall have her hand cut off if she takes hold of her husband by the genitals, even though it be in a case of extremity for the purpose of delivering him from an enemy.

It must not be supposed, however, that this religious reverence for perfect masculinity is confined to the past, for at the present day one who is sexually mutilated, and therefore not "a man," cannot be consecrated as a priest nor promoted to a bishopric ; much less, exalted to the papal throne.

This requirement, that religious teachers and leaders shall possess a generative organism perfect in form and function, is a very general one and always has been, nor is it restricted to persons of that class, but is made a condition precedent for the holding of various other offices of dignity and honor.

A eunuch or impotent man has always been a despised and accursed creature, scorned alike by man and God. In olden times castration was regarded as a punishment far worse than that of death ; a fate that degraded a man below the level of the meanest and lowest brute. The more virile a man was, the greater was the respect he inspired ; and the veneration paid to a god was always proportionate to the sexual abilities ascribed to him. Such deities as were held to be more strongly endowed with virility and whose office pertained more directly to the procreative functions were honored above their fellow gods, and thus it is that the Creator, the almighty and everlasting Producer, has ever been the supreme god. His creative powers are unlimited ; hence, he is the ruler, the master of all other gods and of men.

CHAPTER III.

THE PHALLUS.

The worship of the phallus, the masculine symbol of creation, dates back into the hidden and unknown ages of the past. The earliest records of the Egyptians and the Hindoos refer to phallic worship as an old-established institution, showing that thousands of years before the Christian era it had already given rise to elaborate systems of theology. All of these religions had for their dominant object the worship of the procreative powers of nature as symbolized by the generative organs, which were represented in images and emblems of the greatest diversity and variety.

Prominent among these representations was the phallus, which, in its stricter sense, has reference more to the image of the male organ than to the organ itself. These images, in exact representation of the masculine member, were very common among the ancients. They were made in every conceivable variety of form and size, many of them being molded in plastic material, and others carved from wood, stone and ivory. Sometimes they represented the organ in its passive state, in which form it was generally of diminutive size and worn as an amulet by the women. Such amulets are still common among the phallic worshipers of India, many of them being of minute size and made of gold, silver, ivory, crystal or sacred wood. These are worn upon the arm or breast and in the turban.

The most common form of these phallic images, however, was the realistic representation of the phallus in its upright position, in which shape it was regarded as more clearly exhibiting the divine attribute of the Creator. When used as household idols these images were about life-size, but those employed in religious festivals and in the temples were much exaggerated, reaching sometimes to a height of twenty or thirty feet, with corresponding proportions throughout.

Many of the Greek and Roman temples, in common with those of other nations, were especially dedicated to the phallus, which occupied the most prominent and holy part of the sacred edifice, and received the worship and adoration of the devotees, who presented it with offerings of flowers and wine, and prayed to it as the hallowed representative of the Creator.

This image was a prominent feature in the Bacchanalia and other springtime festivals of the Greeks and Romans, in celebration of the regeneration of life. On these occasions the women repaired to the temples of this idol, and there performed the mysteries connected with its worship as the representative of the Divine Regenerator, singing the while hymns of praise to the deity, and anointing the sacred phallus with consecrated wine, besides wreathing it with flowers and presenting offerings of various kinds.

The Roman Liberalia, which were held in March, were a festive though religious celebration in honor of Liber, another title of Bacchus, the god of generative power. This was an occasion of general rejoicing, and was not confined to a particular place or set of worshipers, as in the case of the Bacchanalian mysteries, but was observed by the people in all parts of Italy and the Roman provinces.

The phallus, as the symbol of Bacchus, played an important part in these festivities. In many places this emblem of regenerated life was placed in a chariot and, covered with flowers and attended by a merry crowd of men, women and children, was drawn about the fields, along the highways and through the towns, amid the rejoicings and acclamations of the people.

In some of the towns and cities, a magnificent car bearing an enormous phallus, gaily decorated, was slowly drawn through the streets, accompanied by a great procession of people, and in this manner was borne to the center of the forum, where it came to a halt. The most respected matron of the town, as worthy of the post of honor, then advanced amid the joyous shouts of the populace, and crowned the symbol of the deity with a wreath of ivy.

The festival of Venus, the goddess of love and regeneration, was celebrated by the Roman women at the same time or soon after the Liberalia. This celebration was attended with rejoicings and merry-making, and a general relaxation of the strict rules of feminine decorum. In the formal ceremonies of the occasion the ladies proceeded in state to the Quirinal, the hill of Romulus, where stood the temple containing the sacred phallus. This holy emblem was taken possession of by the women, who then formed in procession and reverently escorted it to the temple of Venus, where they presented it to that goddess amid elaborate and joyful rites.

This ceremony is illustrated by a design on an old Roman gem, which shows a triumphal chariot bearing an altar upon which rests a colossal phallus. A female figure hovers over this symbol holding a crown of flowers above it. The chariot, which is under a richly-decorated canopy supported by four semi-nude women, is drawn by bulls and goats, ridden by winged children and preceded by a band of women blowing trumpets. At the destination of the procession is a representation of a vulva upheld by two genii. When the ceremony was completed by the union of the two emblems, the phallus was devoutly carried back to its temple.

Smaller images of the phallus were frequently set up by the roadside, in front of the doors of dwellings and beneath the trees in sacred groves and woods. The spot on which this holy emblem stood was regarded as hallowed ground, and the images received the same pious reverence and adoration as is to-day paid to the symbols of Christianity.

No doubt, many of the devotees regarded the phallus as the deity itself, even as is the case with many to-day who pray to the image of the Virgin or the crucified Savior, yet their devotion and piety were none the less deep and sincere. The woman who knelt before the consecrated image of the masculine creative power and prayed for the blessing of children, was as earnest and modest as is the Christian woman of this day who invokes a similar boon from the holy Virgin or the Father.

The chances for securing fruitfulness

were considered better if the prayer was offered while in contact with the image, and for this reason it was customary for the suppliants to bare themselves and sit upon the phallus while praying.

This rite is still practised in certain parts of the world by girls and women of all ages and stations, for the purpose of invoking divine aid. In oriental villages it is common to see two stones—one, flat and circular, the other, small, smooth and upright—standing near together in some secluded nook or grove. The suppliant steps upon the circular stone, adjusts her drapery, and, seating herself upon the upright stone, repeats a short prayer and calls upon her god for some desired blessing.

A writer, who was long a sojourner in India, relates that "Many a day have I sat at early dawn in the door of my tent, pitched in a sacred grove, and gazed at the little group of females stealthily emerge from the adjoining, half-sleeping village, each with a garland or bunch of flowers, and, when none were thought to see, accompany their prayer for pooli-palam (child-fruit) with a respectful abrasion of a certain part of their person on a phallus."

By reason of its sacredness the phallus was considered a charm against evil spirits and it is occasionally found in ancient tombs, where it was placed to guard the dead from the Evil One. A remarkable instance of this custom was discovered not long since in Egypt, where there was found at Thebes the mummy of a woman of rank with whom there was buried the embalmed phallus of a bull.

The use and worship of phallic images is referred to in the most ancient records. In the book of Genesis it is related that when Jacob with his family and flocks left the house of Laban, his wife Rachel carried away with her Laban's terephim, which were small images of men with the phallus constituting the prominent feature. The sacred importance attached to these images is shown by the fact that Laban went after Jacob, and, overtaking his son-in-law at the end of a seven-day's journey, asked, "Wherefore hast thou stolen my gods?" and Jacob, not knowing that his wife had taken them, told Laban that if he found the images on any one of his people, that person should be put to death. In order not to be discovered, Rachel sat upon the idols " and said to her father, Let it not displease my lord that I cannot rise before thee, for the custom of women is upon me. And he searched and found not the images."

Again, in the book of Judges we learn how Micah made some of these images for himself and how the Danites took them from him and worshiped them ; and in the first book of Kings is an account of Maachah, the queen of the Israelites, who was deposed because she made a phallic image and worshiped it.

In fact, the Old Testament contains numerous references to images and idols of this character ; nor must it be supposed that the use of such emblems is peculiar to the remote past ; for, as will be presently shown, they are abundantly general in India and are common in other phallic-worshiping nations of this day ; as in Dahomey, for example, where phallic figures are prominent in the streets of every settlement.

To within a very short time ago they figured prominently in the Christian festival of St. Cosmo and Damiano, at Isernia in Italy, on which occasion phallic images in wax were offered to the priest by the female devotees, accompanied by prayers for matrimonial and maternal blessings. A similar custom prevailed in certain parts of France, where these wax offerings were made to St. Foutin, the patron saint of virility; and as a further evidence of the existence of modified phallic worship in connection with Christianity it is authoritatively related that at Orange, in the church of St. Eutropius, was a phallus made of wood and covered with leather, which was highly venerated by the inhabitants of the town as a symbol of the saint, whose aid was sought in all matters pertaining to the generative functions.

The phallus was frequently pictured on coins and in sculpture and upon vases and other articles, as may be seen in the remains that have been found not only in the ancient cities, but in those of more modern times. Bas-reliefs from some of the old buildings in France show singular varieties of the phallus, some of them double and triple and provided with wings, claws, beaks, etc. One is bridled and ridden by a sprite, another is shown receiving the adoration of female devotees, while still another is depicted standing on human legs. These, as well as those pictured on lamps and vases used for sacerdotal purposes, were designed as symbolical of religious ideas.

Numerous examples of phallic-figured vases and dishes have been found in Rome and other Italian cities. In the museum at Portici, for example, on the cover of an ancient vase that had been used for sacred purposes, is a large phallus which is being embraced by a woman, while another shows a dealer in phalli offering a basketful of his wares to a group of women. While the religious significance of such designs would scarcely be appreciated at this day, the very fact that they were depicted on articles used in the sanctuaries is evidence of the sacred meaning originally attached to them.

Under its Hindu name of *lingam* the phallus is still universally used as a religious symbol throughout India, where phallic worship has flourished unabated for thousands of years. The lingam is the divine symbol of Siva, the Reproducer, the third member of the Hindu creative trinity, and is to be found in every temple dedicated to his worship. It is generally in the sanctum, or holy of holies, and garlanded with flowers or adorned with other offerings. These lingams are made of granite, marble, ivory and precious wood, and are generally of very large size, some reaching to the enormous height of forty feet and measuring twenty-five feet in circumference.

The temples of the lingam are to be seen in great numbers on the banks of the Ganges, especially in the neighborhood of Calcutta. Their presence near the river invests them with greater sanctity than if built in the interior of the country, the river being considered particularly sacred. Connected with nearly every one of these temples is a small house, open in front, for the accommodation of the devotees who come there to die in sight of the river. The temples occur in groups of eight or ten, while at some places as many as a hundred are located within short range of one another.

The priests connected with these temples are sworn to the strictest chastity, and as they are nude while officiating any carnal excitement of the imagination would manifest itself in the external organs and would result in the summary stoning of the unfaithful priest.

While the lingams in the temples are of gigantic proportions, those used for domestic worship are but a few inches in height; and, as before stated, this emblem in diminutive size is worn as an amulet or charm and is used by the Hindoos in prayer as the pious Catholic uses the symbol or image of his patron saint.

The worship of the lingam is an important and necessary religious rite, and when fully and properly performed in accordance with the prescribed ritual, is a very elaborate ceremony, consisting of sixteen essential requisites, including a prefatory bath of purification by the worshiper, the bathing of the lingam with clarified butter, honey and the juice of sugar cane, the offering of flowers, incense, lamps, fruits and various kinds of prepared edibles, the repetition of prayers, and the walking about and bowing before the image.

It is not necessary that this worship should take place in the temple, but may be performed in any purified place. It is considered most efficacious when performed on the bank of a holy river before a lingam formed of clay. The Hindoos of every caste and of both sexes make images of this symbol with the clay of the Ganges, every morning after bathing, and worship before them ; bowing, presenting offerings, and repeating incantations. Upon the completion of the ceremony the image is thrown into the river.

Every village has its public lingam, which is set up in the most conspicuous part of the town as a talisman. It is generally two or three feet in height, and early in the morning may be seen the girls of the neighborhood, who are anxious for husbands, sprinkling the emblem with water from the Ganges, decking it with garlands of flowers, and, while rubbing themselves against it, reciting the prescribed incantations and entreating the deity to make them fruitful mothers.

A common and more realistic method adopted by the ancients for depicting the symbol of the male procreative power was in the statue or representation of the male figure, either entirely nude or simply exhibiting the phallus, which was generally of unnaturally large size. There are to be seen to the present day on the walls of the temples at Karnak and Thebes phallic designs that illustrate how intimately the ideas of sexuality and religion were interwoven in the old Egyptian civilization. There are many figures of their gods and kings showing them possessed of unusual and abundant virility. These pictures also represent the castration of captives, a common method of punishment among the ancients, who regarded the absence of sexual power as the most humiliating disgrace that could befall a man. The

Egyptian god Osiris is very frequently depicted with large and prominent genitals, as a mark of his divine and supreme power, and images of him in this form were carried about in the processions connected with the religious festivals of the Egyptians.

The Roman phallus-god Priapus, the deity of procreation, was always represented by a figure of this kind, and as the Romans were ardent worshipers of Priapus and introduced the worship among the peoples with whom they came in contact, images and statues of this kind are not rare in the various ancient towns of Italy and other parts of Europe. Roman coins, sculpturing, and engraved stones, or gems, abound in representations of Priapus, showing him in all forms and attitudes; sometimes alone, but frequently as the central figure in suggestive scenes or unequivocal sexual pastimes.

These priapic images were objects of reverential worship as realistic representations of the creative deity, and were particularly resorted to by women who desired maternal joys and by newly married women, who were required to sacrifice their virginity to the deity through the medium of his holy image.

So deep was the faith implanted in the common mind regarding the efficacy of prayers addressed to these statues of the creative deity, that the worship of them in certain parts of France continued down to within a comparatively recent time; the only difference in the worship being that the images were given the name of Christian saints instead of their ancient pagan name of Priapus.

At Bourg Dieu, near Bourges, the inhabitants of the town worshiped one of these statues that had existed from the time of the Romans. The monks, fearing to put an end to this old-established religious practice, converted the ancient god into St. Greluchon, and barren women flocked to the abbey to implore the saint's aid and to celebrate a novena in his honor. The devotee would stretch herself at full length on this figure, which was laid upon the floor, and would then scrape some particles from the phallus, and these particles in water were supposed to constitute a miraculous beverage.

St. Giles, in Brittany, St. Réné, in Anjou, and St. Regnaud and St. Arnaud were similarly worshiped; though in the case of the latter a mystic apron usually shrouded the symbol of fecundity, and was only raised in favor of sterile devotees. Its mere inspection, if accompanied with true faith, was said to be sufficient to effect miracles.

St. Foutin was one of the most popular of the saints to whom were ascribed the power of procreation. Statues to him were common in various parts of France, and he was the recipient of many prayers and offerings, for he was said to have not only the gift of relieving barren women, but of restoring exhausted vitality and curing secret diseases. His worship, therefore, was not confined to the female devotees, but was shared equally by the men, who would devoutly present to the priests, as offerings to the saint, wax images of the affected parts, in the pious and sincere belief that by this holy means they would be cured.

Among the remains of a church at Embrun was found the phallus of a statue of this saint, which was stained a deep red as the result of the custom of pouring wine upon it. The anointment of the image in this manner was a common practice in connection with the worship of the saint; the wine thus used being caught in a jar and allowed to turn sour, when, under the name of "holy vinegar," it was drunk by the women as an effective and infallible means of producing fertility.

CHAPTER IV.

PHALLIC EMBLEMS.

While statues of Priapus and images of the phallus are found in great abundance in the remains of the ancient world, and while they were no doubt extensively used at all times, they cannot compare in numbers and importance with the modified and conventional forms of the creative symbol that we find scattered all over the world, in endless numbers and variety, and unknowingly preserved by us to-day in our architecture, our symbols and our customs. Realistic representations of the masculine generative symbol became very readily modified into more formal shapes, which were adopted and retained, either for the sake of convenience, because they could be more easily made, or for the reason that they could be better adapted to certain ceremonial uses.

Pre-eminent among this class of phallic emblems is the pillar. It is not difficult to understand how the large upright phallus became modified into the conventional form of a pillar. In fact, many of the large phalli were really nothing more than pillars, and hence a plain pillar, either of wood or stone, was adopted as a symbol of the procreative power. It was easily, cheaply and readily constructed, and as its general form was plainly suggestive of the object it represented, it is not surprising that it became one of the most popular and most numerous of phallic emblems.

Remains of stone pillars as symbols of the deity are found in all parts of the world. They are numerous throughout Europe, the British Isles and America, while in Egypt and in India and other Asiatic countries, they abound in the greatest profusion. The marvelous Egyptian obelisks are nothing more nor less than large pillars, phallic emblems, erected in honor of the Creator and his divine attribute. Indeed, all ancient structures of this kind—pillars, columns, obelisks and monuments—are of phallic significance and owe their existence to religious motives and the devout endeavor on the part of mankind to honor the Creator.

The use of the pillar in one form or another was very extensive. Remains of this emblem in all parts of Europe and in England, Scotland and Ireland bear evidence of the fact that phallic worship was not confined to certain localities or peoples, but was general and played a dominant part in the religion of the Scandinavians, the Teutons, the Saxons, the Celts, the Gauls, and the Britons, besides that of the Romans and the Greeks. To catalogue and explain the monuments and remains of phallicism that have been found in Great Britain would alone require a large volume.

Stone phalli in the form of pillars are common in the temples of China and Japan, and, in fact, among all the oriental nations. Passing to the western hemisphere, we find that phallicism, as represented by this emblem, was almost universal among the primitive and prehistoric races of both continents. In Yucatan a phallic pillar stands in front of the door of every temple. In Peru have been found numerous examples of this symbol, together with ancient clay phalli, and water jars on which are figured gods and goddesses of procreation; their functions and attributes being prominently portrayed. In the center of the great square of the temple of the sun at Cuzco the early European explorers found a stone idol, shaped like a sugar loaf and covered with gold leaf, which was the object of special veneration on the part of the populace; and in Brazil have been found similar indications of the primitive worship of the generative powers.

In Polynesia pillars are made of straw, a custom which is also practised in India, especially in harvest time, when pillars and human figures exhibiting both sexes very conspicuously are made and set up in the fields as objects of adoration and worship.

In ancient times stone pillars were erected at the cross roads, at boundaries, in the market places, before the doors of houses and in the temples and churches, as the presence of this holy emblem was supposed to consecrate the place in which it stood, and to guard it against evil spirits. For a similar reason stone pillars and shafts (symbols of the guardian Creator) were placed upon graves,—a practice that has been retained to this day in the civilized world ; for do we not continue to mark the resting-places of our departed ones with monuments and columns and other upright stones ?

We have ample proof in the Bible that the pillar was regarded as a sacred emblem of the Creator, for it will be remembered that the setting up of a pillar as a witness to the Lord was a common practice among the Hebrews, and that it was always an occasion of reverential ceremonies. "In that day there shall be an altar to the Lord in the midst of the land of Egypt, and a pillar at the border thereof to the Lord ; and it shall be for a sign and for a witness unto the Lord." (Isaiah 19 : 19.)

Those acquainted with the Old Testament cannot but be impressed with the sacredness attached to pillars, and the numerous instances in which they are mentioned in connection with the Lord, either as emblems of the Creator or as witnesses to him. They are frequently referred to as altars and rocks, which, as will presently be shown, are but modified forms of the pillar, and equally significant.

Jacob set up a pillar and poured oil upon it, calling the place Bethel,—the house of God. He also set up a stone pillar, in obedience to God's command to build an altar, and poured upon it oil and a drink offering of wine; a common method of anointing phallic symbols, and practised by the people of all nations when making offerings to the creative deity. Likewise, when his wife Rachel died he set a pillar upon her grave, in accordance with the custom previously alluded to.

We find, also, that Joshua, when about to die, took a great stone and set it up under an oak that was near the sanctuary of the Lord, " and Joshua said unto all the people, Behold, this stone shall be a witness unto us, for it hath heard all the words of the Lord which he spake unto us: it shall be therefore a witness unto you, lest ye deny your God." The Lord looked upon the Egyptians through a pillar of fire; he led the Israelites by pillars of cloud and fire, and he appeared to them in a pillar of cloud ;—records that are all illustrative of the divine significance of the pillar.

Not only was this emblem recognized and used as significant of the Creator, but the Lord is frequently alluded to as a Pillar, or a Rock; showing conclusively the sacred meaning attached to the symbol. Thus, Jacob refers to Jehovah as " The Stone of Israel ;" while David calls him his " Rock," and Moses several times uses this emblematical term ; its phallic significance being especially clear in the 18th verse of the thirty-second chapter of Deuteronomy, where he says : " Of the Rock that begat thee thou art unmindful, and hast forgotten God that formed thee." Equally clear is the expression of Hannah, who in her prayer of thanksgiving to the Lord for having given her a child, says : " Neither is there any Rock like our God."

As the vast majority of pillars were made of stone, or consisted simply of unhewn rocks set up on end, it is not difficult to perceive how the " rock " and the " pillar " became interchangeable terms; the one as symbolical and significant as the other. By an extension of the analogy, mere stones, without any particular likeness to pillars, became emblematical of the Creator, especially when piled in a heap; such stone heaps being a very common form of the phallic symbol. In the thirty-first chapter of Genesis we read that "Jacob took a stone and set it up for a pillar, and Jacob said unto his brethren, Gather stones; and they took stones and made an heap. And Laban said to Jacob, Behold this heap, and behold this pillar. This heap be a witness and this pillar be a witness," etc.

On the other hand, the altar was an elaboration of the pillar; a change that resulted from the practice of making offerings to the phallus or pillar that was in the temple. In the desire to place the offerings upon the sacred symbol, its form was gradually modified so as to better accommodate them, and the result was the altar; an object still regarded with holy reverence, and still forming the principal feature of every place of worship.

As in the case of the altar, so the pillar became modified in various other ways, one of which resulted in giving to the pole a sacred and phallic significance. In fact, our word *pole* is derived from *phallus*, which is itself a derivative of the Phenician word meaning "he breaks through or passes into." The modern Maypole festivities are simply a continuation of some ancient phallic celebration, in which the pole, as a symbol of the reproductive powers, was decorated with flowers, while the worshipers danced about it singing songs of joy and praise.

The principal outgrowth of the pillar was the tower. In truth, this symbol was but a further enlargement and elaboration of the phallus image. In addition to consecrating a temple of worship by placing within it a symbol of the Deity, the temple itself was built in the shape of the symbol, as far as possible, and this resulted in the erection of towers; remains of which are still to be seen in various parts of the world, especially in Great Britain. They were built of stone, and because of their circular shape are to-day known as "Round Towers," the most noteworthy examples of which are those found in Ireland, where these ancient phallic structures abound in great numbers, having been built by phallic-worshiping refugees from ancient Persia. These towers vary in height from fifty to one hundred and fifty feet, measuring about fourteen feet in diameter at the base, and decreasing gradually toward the top. Some are surmounted with a conical-shape roof, while others terminate in a point, and thus resemble huge steeples standing alone. But in all their variety of forms, the suggestiveness of their design is always evident.

We have every evidence that such phallic towers were common in all parts of the ancient world; but in course of time these necessarily circumscribed edifices gave place to more commodious forms of architecture, though the tower in some one of its various forms was always retained as the principal and consecratory feature of a religious building; and to this day, throughout all Christendom, the houses of religious worship are distinguished in this manner.

A church is not considered complete without its steeple or tower, but little is it realized that this important and distinguishing feature of church architecture is a representation of the primitive symbol of the Creator, and that its original function was to hallow the place in which the deity of procreation was worshiped. In no ancient city could the phallic symbols of the Almighty have been more prominently and widely displayed than they are to-day in every Christian town, with its multitude of lofty steeples and spires towering above the housetops, in glorious, though unconscious, symbolization of the Creator.

Many other artificial and conventional emblems used in ancient times for the representation of the procreative deity might be cited; as the arrow, the shepherd's crook, the three-pointed wand, which has become the fleur-de-lis of modern times, and a great many more; but they are of minor importance compared with the pillar and the tower, and with the numerous natural objects that were chosen as phallic symbols by reason of some supposed resemblance or relation to the phallus, in its looks, character or attributes. Thus, any high rock, or mount, or other towering elevation was vested with sacred significance, and ancient history abounds with references to "holy mounts," or "mounts of God."

Trees, too, were regarded as sacred emblems of the Creator and his attributes. Some, like the pine and the fir, because of their straightness and uprightness; others, like the oak, because of their strength and vitality; and others, again, like the fig and the palm, because of the shape of their leaves or the venereal effect of their fruit. Hence, we find that tree worship, as a mode of phallicism, flourished very extensively in the early history of the world; the worship of the oak by the Druids being a familiar example, and all early records contain allusions to certain kinds of trees and fruits as possessed of particular religious or phallic significance.

Various animals were likewise adopted as suggestive symbols of the male creative energy, particularly those of unusual sexual power. The cock, the goat and the bull figure very largely in phallic worship as worthy representatives of the procreative god ; the goat and the bull being especially sacred to the Egyptians, who looked upon these animals as not only the living symbols of Osiris, the Creator, but as his actual incarnations, and were accordingly treated and worshiped as veritable deities. The sacred bull, as an incarnation of the procreative power of nature, is a feature of many of the Hindoo temples, where the animal is waited upon and adored with due reverence and solemnity.

The goat is perhaps the most salacious of all animals, his inexhaustible appetite and virility enabling him to mate with as many as eighty ewes in a single night, and it is not surprising that such extraordinary abilities should have appealed to the impressible mind of early man as a manifestation of the infinite powers of the Supreme Procreator himself, and that he should have been chosen as a specially sacred symbol.

This animal figured very prominently in many of the religious celebrations, and down to the present time has been employed in the initiation ceremonies of secret orders, as he was in the mystic rites of the ancient Egyptians, in which the priests were required to be initiated into the mysteries of the Goat before they could be admitted to the divine knowledge of Isis. These mysteries were so sacred and so zealously guarded by the few initiates, that very little is really known concerning them.

The Greeks idealized the goat in their god Pan and his voluptuous attendants, the fauns and satyrs; creatures half man and half goat. Pan was the patron deity of sensual pastimes, and representations of him depict him as worthy of the highest honor on this score.

Among the Hindoos the tortoise is an important phallic emblem. This animal was probably chosen as a sacred representative of the creative deity because of its fabled androgyny,— an attribute of the Creator which will be considered in another place,— and because of its great tenacity of life and fecundity. Furthermore, the frequency and rapidity with which it protrudes and withdraws its head, changing from an appearance of repose to one of energy and action, as well as the shape of its head and neck when aroused, readily suggested to the imaginative phallic-worshiper the active lingam, or masculine creative symbol.

Among the more important natural emblems adopted by the Egyptians was the river Nile, which symbolized the outpouring, the fertilizing and creative force, of Osiris, and its waters were regarded with the same holy veneration that characterizes the worship of the river Ganges by the people of India to-day.

But foremost of all natural emblems of the creative deity was the sun; nay, the sun was the Creator himself, the Almighty God. It was he who gave light and life to the world; upon him all existence depended. Osiris dwelt in the Sun as the omnipotent Creator, and through this all-potent medium manifested his powers to mankind. All of the ancient supreme gods were closely allied with the sun. It was either the Deity himself or his glorious and almighty manifestation. The worship of the sun, therefore, necessarily formed a part,— a very important and significant part,— of phallic worship. In the adoration of the sun as the Creator and Preserver of mankind lies the origin of a universal theological belief,—a belief that belongs to no one sect or age alone, but has been in existence and has been the foundation of religious faiths since the time man first beheld the wonders of the universe, and watched with anxious and reverential solicitude the annual journey of the Sun; saw with dismay and fear the world grow cold and dead in the absence of the great Life-giver in the winter season, and welcomed with joy and acclamations of praise the renewal, the resurrection of life, as the Sun, the Almighty Father and Savior, appeared again in all his glory and radiance of power.

CHAPTER V.

SEXUAL SACRIFICES.

While the world at large has always regarded sexual power or virility as a divine gift, to be cherished and exercised in accordance with its sacred and mysterious purpose, and has looked upon the act of generation as not only proper and necessary, but as a holy and divinely ordained function for the accomplishment of the supreme purpose of life, there has always been in human society a small but powerful religious element that insists upon an abnegation of the sexual nature, as the only true condition for a proper communion with God.

Hence, we find in all times and among all peoples certain religious cults whose priests or leaders are required to abstain from all sexual affairs. Among the ancients this rule was not confined to mere continence or celibacy, but was often extended to actual emasculation of the priests; a custom that attained its greatest prominence in Phrygia, an ancient province of Asia Minor, because of the extraordinary ceremonies there attendant upon the act of castration. These ceremonies formed a part of the annual celebration of the festival of Attis and Cybele; the latter being the earth goddess or mother deity, who fell in love with the beautiful youth Attis, of whom she exacted a vow of chastity as her priest, but who, having broken his vow for the sake of a lovely nymph, was deprived by the goddess of his reason, and in his frenzy he castrated himself; whereupon the goddess ordained that thereafter all her priests should be eunuchs.

In commemoration of this legend, there was held each year, in the springtime, a wild and noisy though at the same time sacred and solemn festival. It began in quiet and sorrow for the death-like sleep of Attis. On the third day joy broke forth and was manifested by delirious hilarity. The frenzied priests of Cybele rushed about in bands, with haggard eyes and disheveled hair, like drunken revelers and insane women. In one hand they carried burning fire-brands and in the other they brandished the sacred knife. They dashed into the woods and valleys and climbed the mountain heights, keeping up a horrible noise and continual groaning. An intoxicating drink rendered them wild. They beat each other with the chains they carried, and when they drew blood upon their companions or themselves they danced with wild and tumultuous gesticulations, flogging their backs and piercing their limbs and even their bodies. Finally, in honor of their goddess, they turned the sacred knife upon their genitals, and calling upon their deity showed their gaping wounds, and offered her the spoils of their destroyed virility. After recovering from this self-inflicted emasculation, these initiates adopted woman's dress, and were then ready to become priests or, failing in that, to take their place among the attendants of the temple, to engage in pederasty for the benefit of the temple treasury, whenever the patrons might prefer such indulgence to that afforded by the consecrated women.

The motive for sexual sacrifices of this kind is probably to be found in the desire to resemble the Deity in his androgynous character. As will be shown, there were numerous religious faiths in which it was held that the creative deity combined in himself both the male and female principles, and as the ultimate aim of the priesthood has ever been to attain to a resemblance to or a union with God, it is but reasonable that such a method should have been adopted by certain sects. A castrated priest was neither man nor woman ; and yet, paradoxically, he was both. In form and figure he represented the male principle, while in dress and in the absence of the active masculine functions, he represented the female.

In some instances, however, and particularly in later times, this motive gave place to one of another character, and this was the desire to please and propitiate the Almighty by sacrificing the greatest of human blessings and pleasures, in accordance with the old and widespread belief that God is always best pleased when his creatures are most miserable; and hence, the greater the sacrifice, the greater the pleasure afforded him.

Castration is practised by many religious fanatics even at the present day, and is prescribed as a fundamental tenet of a certain sect of Christians in Russia, who hold that the millennium will not arrive until all the men of the world are castrated. Consequently, this sect is composed entirely of self-made eunuchs, and hundreds of converts annually butcher themselves in this manner. Their authority for this practice is found in the twelfth verse of the nineteenth chapter of Matthew, wherein Christ says unto his disciples, "There are some eunuchs which were so born from their mother's womb; and there are some eunuchs which were made eunuchs of men; and there be eunuchs which have made themselves eunuchs for the kingdom of heaven's sake."

In the history of Christianity this passage has not infrequently been the inciting cause of sexual sacrifices, but the chief motive for sacrifices of this nature has been the endeavor to give up all worldly delights and vain enjoyments, as incompatible with a proper worship of God. Hence, the struggles of the early Christian fathers and devotees and of the many who have followed in their footsteps down to the present day, to resist the promptings of the flesh, in order to attain to a pure, spiritual communion with God.

This did not necessarily imply castration; yet there were many (among whom was Origen, one of the most famous of the early fathers) who resorted to it as the only means of successfully subduing the temptations of the devil. The majority sought to accomplish their purpose by taking vows of absolute continence; and the greater the struggles they endured, the greater was their triumph and spiritual satisfaction. That the faithful did suffer by thus absolutely abstaining from the gratification of their natural desires and appetites, is well attested by history and by the well-known physiological fact, that absolute continence is attended with mental and physical derangements as painful and as disastrous as those resulting from the most intemperate indulgence.

This mode of sexual sacrifice, in its modified form of celibacy, as a sacerdotal requirement, still constitutes a prominent feature of the tenets and church government of a large part of the Christian world.

Sexual offerings to the deities were not confined alone to masculine devotees, for it was a common religious ordinance in many of the ancient nations, that every woman should sexually sacrifice herself to the gods; not, however, by any act of mutilation, but by permitting herself to be embraced by a patron of the temple.

Whenever a woman desired to perform this religious duty she repaired to the temple and placed herself under a suspended branch of mistletoe, which was the customary mode of indicating that she was at the service of the first stranger who desired to take advantage of the opportunity ; a custom which, in its modified form of kissing under the mistletoe, is retained to this day and is familiar to all of us as a feature of Christmas festivities.

The temple of Mylitta, at Babylon, was particularly noted for the sacrifices of this kind that were made there, and the following account of the manner in which the rites were conducted is taken from the description given by Herodotus:

"Every native-born woman is obliged at sometime in her life to go to the Temple of Mylitta and submit her person to the embraces of a strange man. Many of the more wealthy, who disdain to be confounded with the commonalty, have themselves carried to the temple in covered chairs. There they keep their seats with a following of many domestics who have accompanied them. But the majority of the women, who wear on their heads a circlet made of cord, settle themselves in a certain part of the grounds that pertain to the temple. There is a constant stream of women arriving and departing. The men strangers walk up and down the passageways formed by stretched ropes, and pick out the women who best please them. A woman having once entered cannot return home until a man, with whom she has had no carnal intercourse before, kneels and throws to her a piece of silver, exclaiming as he does so, 'I invoke the goddess Mylitta!'—this being the Assyrian name for Venus;—and however trifling the sum thrown to her may be, its refusal would be unlawful, because the silver so offered becomes sacred and is applied to religious purposes. The woman is obliged, therefore, to follow him, and the two repair at once to one of the semi-secluded alcoves of the temple designed for the purpose in view. At length, having performed her duty to the goddess, she returns home and cannot be again subjected to the ordeal, whatever may be the sum of money offered her. Those who are fortunate enough to be pretty or elegantly dressed do not remain long in the temple. The ugly and otherwise less-favored must stay longer, because they are not able to so readily fulfill their mission, and for this reason some have been obliged to dwell there for three or four years."

This practice resembled that of the consecrated prostitution so common among phallic-worshiping people, in the fact that sexual union under these divine auspices was considered both proper and holy, but its object was, of course, different from that which governed the profession of the women of the temple. In the vast majority of cases, the women who thus presented themselves at the temples were maidens, whose purpose it was to sacrifice their virginity to the patron deity.

From time immemorial virginity has been regarded as divinely sacred, and has universally been looked upon as belonging exclusively to the gods. This belief was so strongly implanted in the minds of the ancient Romans, that their law would not permit a virgin to be executed in the ordinary manner. No matter what the enormity of her guilt, the woman, if a virgin, could not be subjected to the penalty of death by violent hands. By reason of her virginity she was the property of the gods; she contained within her the spiritual presence of the Deity; and hence, before inflicting the last penalty, it was the duty of the executioner to remove the god from her, and for this purpose he was obliged, as a part of his office, to deflower her; after which she was strangled or burned.

This idea of the holiness of maidenhood led to the adoption of religious precepts requiring that virginity should be given to God, and to this day such sacrifices are made in all parts of the civilized world by Christian women who take solemn vows of chastity, and confine themselves in convents, for the purpose of giving up their lives and their virginity to the Almighty.

Among the ancients, however, life-long continence was not regarded as a necessary means for the sacrifice of virginity. The religious duty of women to bear children would not in those days have permitted such a custom. To them it was sufficient that the first sexual act of a woman should be given to her deity; that the act by which she gave up her divine virginity should be dedicated to the god or goddess of her religion. This was sometimes done in the manner as described by Herodotus, but among other peoples it was deemed essential that the sacrifice should be made through a holy representative of the deity or by means of his consecrated image.

Accordingly, we find that in some cases it was customary for women to give up their virginity to the priests of the temples, while others offered their maidenhood to an image of the Creator. This latter mode was common in Rome, where the marriage laws required that before the nuptials could be consummated, the bride must sacrifice her virginity to Priapus. It was usual, therefore, immediately after the conclusion of the wedding ceremonies, for the bride and her husband, attended by the parents and friends, to repair to a statue of Priapus, and there, in the presence of her husband and the assembled company, take her first lesson in practical priapic worship by means of the iron or stone phallus of the sacred image.

This rite was a solemnly religious one. The bride was thus brought to the priapic statue immediately after the wedding, in order not only that she should give to the god his due, but that she might be rendered fruitful by contact with the divine generator and be capable of faithfully and well performing all the duties of her untried situation as a wife. The ceremony was accompanied with an offering of flowers and libations of wine and with prayers to the god for matrimonial and maternal blessings.

CHAPTER VI.

THE FEMALE PRINCIPLE.

A far greater importance has always been attached to the male than to the female principle of creation. The Creator always was and ever has been regarded as masculine. The supreme god of every theology is a male. This is due to the fact that the part played by the woman in the phenomenon of procreation is not only passive and receptive, but was for a long time regarded as merely functional. The woman was simply the man's chattel, whose only purpose was to bear him his children. That she contributed toward the production of the offspring by any creative power of her own was not appreciated. Only the masculine—the active—element was recognized in the act of procreation; it alone was the generator. The female element was naught but that of a passive producer and bearer of what the male created.

But in time mankind awoke to a realization of the fact that the female element

THE FEMALE PRINCIPLE.

plays an important and essential part in the reproduction of life; that not only is the union of the sexes necessary for procreation, but that the production of the offspring depends upon the co-operation and reciprocal activity of both elements, and hence the female principal of nature, instead of being considered simply as a passive medium, was exalted and worshiped as a potent factor in the mystery of creation and reproduction.

In fact, there were some among the early people of the world who carried this worship to an extreme, holding that the female creative power was superior to that of the male, and that the feminine generative organs were the true symbol of the creative deity. This gave rise to two great religious factions: the worshipers of the female symbol, the yoni, and the worshipers of the phallus or lingam. In the very oldest records of the world there are certain vague allusions here and there to great religious wars of prehistoric times—wars between the Yonites and the Lingamites; wars that were more terrible and destructive than any that have shaken the world in later times and whose fundamental issue was never settled, but has descended from age to age and from generation to generation, even unto this day, where we find man still fighting and ready to fight, to prove that his god is the only true god.

Our earliest records and traditions indicate, however, that a reconciliatory worship of both the male and female principles had become general thousands of years ago; for we find in all religions a reverential recognition of the necessity of female co-operation in the production of life. Although the Creator, the Supreme God, is always represented as masculine and omnipotent, it is also true that in no theological account of the genesis of the world is it held that the Creator brought life into existence without the assistance of the feminine element. In some of the old theologies, as the Greek and Egyptian, for example, the Creator is represented with a consort, a celestial wife, who was worshiped as next in rank to the Creator himself.

Again, as in the case of Brahma, the supreme god of the Hindoos, he is represented as androgynous; that is, uniting both sexes in one and being thus capable of sexual union within himself. This idea of an androgynous deity is a very common one in the ancient faiths, as well as among the Hindoos of to-day, and there are found frequent realistic representations of deities possessed of the organs of both sexes, or showing a beard on the face of a goddess, as may be seen in some of the pictures of Venus. Portrayals of the androgynal deity are frequent on the temples of India, and many of the figures are most elaborately designed, in an attempt to both truly and symbolically represent the divine duality of the Creator.

In one of the sacred books of the Hindoos we are told, that "the Supreme Spirit in the act of creation became two-fold; the right side was male, the left side female." The principal symbol in representation of this double-sex divinity is one of a figure made up of male and female parts, but so embellished with mystical designs and symbolical details as to be beyond the comprehension of the average mind ; which, indeed, is the very purpose of this sacred symbol ; for, as the Hindoos say, "When one can interpret this emblem of the androgynous divinity he knows all that is known."

In other theologies, while there is lacking a feminine consort, in the shape of a goddess, or a creator possessed of both sexes, it is recorded that life was brought into existence by the divine impregnation of the earth or the waters, which is virtually a union of the two elements ; for, as will be shown hereafter, both the earth and the waters have always been regarded as feminine and as symbols of the female creative function. In the Mosaic account of genesis we read that "the spirit of the Lord moved upon the face of the waters;" which means, literally, that the Creator impregnated the waters, or the female element of nature.

In short, the human mind could not conceive of creation or reproduction without the employment of both the male and female elements, notwithstanding that the true importance of the latter was sometimes almost entirely ignored, and was worshiped to a much less extent than the former.

That life could be produced without the congress of the two sexes was never believed, for we see that the Almighty and Supreme God could not himself accomplish it. This conviction is further illustrated in the various legends concerning the birth of a god by a virgin. In all of the theologies containing this feature (and there are none that do not), it is taught that the Supreme Father had actual, material knowledge of the virgin; it is not held that she conceived without contact with the masculine element. This, according to universal belief, would have been impossible, in spite of the omnipotence of the Deity; such an occurrence would be contrary to nature and to God.

The holiness and wonder of the birth of a son by a virgin lay not in the fact that a virgin conceived, but that she conceived through the divine impregnation of God; that the Almighty had chosen her for his sacred purpose. Unions between gods and women are frequently related in the ancient mythologies, and are always regarded as sanctifying the woman, of elevating her above her fellow mortals, and of endowing her child with god-like attributes; as witness the legends of the Greek and Roman mythologies, and the account of the immaculate conception and birth of Krishna, the Hindoo saviour, and of Buddha, the founder of one of the greatest religious faiths in the world.

Whatever may be the spiritual idea at the present time regarding the immaculate impregnation of the Virgin of Christianity, it is certain, according to statements in the Bible, that neither Joseph nor Mary, nor, in fact, the writers of the gospels themselves, ever supposed that a woman could conceive without direct masculine assistance. That this idea was held in the church for centuries afterwards is realistically demonstrated by the picture of the "Rosary of the Blessed Virgin," printed by authority of the Church, at Venice, in 1542. This represents the Virgin kneeling before an altar, with her arms and eyes upraised to heaven, where she beholds a radiant throng of cherubim with the Holy Dove in their midst, while a potent ray of light descends and enters her person, on the front of which is a picture of the divinely and miraculously conceived Christ-child.

This universally recognized necessity for the union of the male with the female power, in order to accomplish the glorious purpose of reproduction, naturally resulted in the worship of the female principle as co-ordinate with that of the male, as is found in many of the early religions. Isis, the great feminine creative god of the Egyptians, was worshiped with a veneration fully equal to that bestowed upon her masculine companion, Osiris, and though all nations did not give to the feminine deity so high a rank, there were none that did not have their Goddess of Life, their Queen of Heaven, their Friga, their Aphrodite, or one of a great variety of forms and names under which the deification of the feminine principle was known.

While mankind came to realize the vast significance of the feminine nature and to worship it as a factor in the divine purpose of all life, he did not, as a rule, give to it equal rank with that of the great male principle. The masculine Creator has always been supreme in his power and capabilities. The initiative of all life and activity rests with him; he is the active, moving, generating power of nature, while the female is the receptive, passive element, the molder and preserver of life.

As there were in prehistoric times, so are there to-day certain sects that consider and worship the female principle as superior to that of the male. These are the Hindoo worshipers of Sacti, the supreme feminine creative deity, whose worship consists in the adoration of the vulva as her sacred symbol and divine incarnation. In adoring her mentally the worshiper is taught to imagine this symbol, which is commonly called the *yoni*, in which he must see a chapel, which he is to enter and wherein he is to worship.

The principal ceremony of this sect consists in a religious service designed for the purpose of manifesting reverence for and paying tribute to the divine female power.

This ceremony requires the presence of a young, beautiful and nude girl as a living representative of the goddess. She is generally chosen from the company of consecrated nautch girls attached to the temple, and one thus selected esteems it a special honor, as a tribute to her beauty, accomplishments and abilities, which must be of the highest order to render her worthy as a representative of the immaculate deity. To this girl meat and wine are offered by the devotees, after which follow dancing and the chanting of hymns. As an act of the highest devotion and as typical of the divine means by which life is produced, the devout worshipers conclude the ceremony by a sexual offering to the sacred representative of the deity, who is obliged to bestow her favors upon all of the devotees who desire thus to pay homage to their creator.

The ancient holy regard for the feminine power was in a measure due to its magical and inciting effect upon the masculine nature. It was through the woman that the divine sexual emotions were aroused ; it was the sight or thought of her that brought into activity man's generative nature and powers. The invigorating and inspiring effect produced by the sight or touch of a woman, especially a virgin in the garb of nature, was regarded with deepest reverence as a manifestation of the divine feminine power. Its potency was universally recognized, and we are told that it was employed for the purpose of infusing life and vigor into king David, after he had become aged. "Now king David was old and stricken in years, and they covered him with clothes, but he gat no heat. Wherefore his servants said unto him, Let there be sought for my lord a young virgin; and let her stand before the king, and let her cherish him, and let her lie in thy bosom, that my lord may get heat."

Like those of the masculine principle, the attributes of the feminine element of mankind and of nature were ascribed to a deity, the feminine ruler and patron of fecundity and generation, of sexual power and of love; and the organ (the yoni) through which her powers were manifested became her sacred symbol and was worshipped in the same light and with the same veneration as the phallus. In itself, however, it was regarded with greater reverence than its masculine counterpart; it was more carefully concealed, and treated as more mystical. The sight of a living yoni, particularly that of a virgin, was thought to be of magical virtue, and was considered a certain omen of good fortune.

A remnant of the devout regard formerly inspired by this representative of the feminine deity is still to be found among certain sects in India, Palestine and parts of Africa. The devotee, on bended knee and in silent prayer, offers to the uncovered yoni a part of the food given him by the woman, before he tastes it, which she accepts and eats as evidence of its purity from poison. This ceremony is simply a solemn method of vowing mutual friendship and is similar in meaning to the ancient mode of swearing by grasping the phallus.

CHAPTER VII.

FEMININE EMBLEMS.

The independent yoni, the feminine symbol of creation, was naturally more difficult to exactly represent in the form of an image than was the phallus, or lingam ; and from the very beginning, therefore, this symbol was portrayed in more or less conventional forms and was not infrequently extended to other more easily represented portions of the female anatomy, as the breasts, the *mons Veneris*, etc.

The principal design in representation of the yoni was one that was known under the name of Asherah, which is translated and referred to in the Bible as the " grove," or " groves." This image, which was a symbol of Ashtoreth or of the union of Baal and Ashtoreth—the male and female procreative deities of the Assyrians,—was generally made of wood and had in its center an opening or fissure, which was regarded as preeminently sacred as the Door of Life.

Above this fissure was an emblematical representation of the clitoris, divided into seven parts, and around the Door of Life were carved tufts of hair, thirteen in number, indicating the annual fertile periods of a woman.

Designs of this image occur very frequently in the sculptures of Nineveh and Babylon. It is almost always shown receiving the adoration of the king and his attendants, who hold in their hands pine cones and other symbolical sex offerings. Above the grove is a winged figure—the celestial bowman, with his bow and a quiver full of arrows, for the use of all who desire divine vigor in the concluding rites of the worship, which required that the devotees should unite in sexual congress, as a fitting tribute to the deity; a performance that took place in a small bower situated near the idol.

In the figure and office of the Assyrian bowman we see the prototype of the Grecian Cupid, the little god of love, or amatory desire, with his bow and arrows; the arrow being a very old phallic emblem.

According to the Old Testament, the Israelites were constantly lapsing into idolatry by serving Baal and the groves. Many of their kings deserted the faith of their fathers by building altars, temples and images and burning incense to the phallic deities of the Chaldeans, Assyrians, Egyptians and others. They were particularly persistent in the worship of the groves, " which were set up on every high hill and under every green tree." These were usually surrounded with hangings or curtains, forming a tent or semi-secluded bower, to which the male and female devotees repaired for the sexual consummation of their worship, after having anointed the image and placing before it offerings of fruits, flowers and incense, accompanied with prayers and the chanting of hymns.

Judging from the lamentations of the prophets, and their allusions to some of the practices indulged in by the children of Israel, it is evident that the worship of Baal and other phallic deities of the neighboring tribes was of an intensely sexual character and appealed more strongly to the religious disposition of those days than did the more temperate worship prescribed by the laws of Moses. For a graphic description of the "abominations" resulting from the religious intercourse of the Jews with the Assyrians, Chaldeans and Babylonians, the reader is referred to the 16th and the 23d chapters of Ezekiel.

The most common form of the feminine symbol was that made in representation of the *mons Veneris*. This was represented by mounds and pyramids, remains of which in various styles and sizes are to be found in all parts of the world; the most conspicuous examples being the pyramids of Egypt, which are still the wonder of the world, though comparatively few people recognize or are aware of the religious and sexual significance of these marvelous structures.

They were erected in honor of the feminine creative deity, and no other motive but that of religion could have prompted the building of such gigantic monuments. Various explanations of their purpose and significance have been set forth, with the result that we have been taught to regard them simply as tombs or as great observatories, as though the ancients had nothing better to do or had no higher motives than to build these wonderful structures for the sole purpose of sepulchers, or to scatter observatories all over the country, and many of them within close range of one another.

When we consider that the pyramid of Cheops, for example, covers an area of nearly fourteen acres, that it was originally four hundred and seventy-nine feet in height and contained ninety million cubic feet of rock, which is in immense blocks, each of which had to be quarried, dressed and carried to the pyramid, and this in an age (three thousand years before Christ) when mechanical contrivances were of the most primitive kind,—when these facts are borne in mind, it is irrational to suppose that this titanic work was designed for an insignificant purpose.

It is true that all the pyramids of Egypt were intended for sepulchres, but their shape and colossal proportions were the result of a religious desire to honor the deity and to sanctify the resting-places of the dead by building them in the form of the divine emblem.

Pyramids, or their remains, are likewise met with in Babylon, in various parts of Italy and India, and in China and Japan. Next to Egypt they are most frequent in Mexico and other portions of America. Some of these ancient Mexican pyramids far exceed in area the dimensions of the largest Egyptian monuments, but, unlike those of Egypt, were generally designed for use as temples, though their religious significance and symbolical purpose were the same.

The pyramid was the elaborated or conventionalized form of the mound, the primitive symbol of the *mons Veneris*. Remains of artificial mounds as religious emblems are common in many parts of the world; but, as a rule, greater reverence was paid to natural mounds and elevations, especially those of well-defined shape. Such elevations, therefore, were regarded as sacred spots and were dedicated to divine worship; altars and temples being considered more holy if placed upon a mound, and we learn from the Old Testament how intimately the "high places" and "high hills" were associated with the worship of the feminine deity.

This regard for natural elevations frequently extended to mountains, and there are sects to this day who worship mountains as symbols of the feminine creative deity. In Germany is the famous Hörselberg, commonly called Venusberg, or mountain of Venus. This is the mountain connected with the legend of Tannhäuser, and those who are acquainted with the legend will perceive the full significance of the name given the mountain. In ancient times it was held in particular veneration, not only because of its shape, but because of the large cavern that opens into it.

A natural opening was always looked upon as a particularly sacred emblem. Any hole or cave, any cleft or fissure, any natural crevice, was regarded with holy reverence, as sacred to the divine Mother Earth. From time immemorial the earth has been regarded as feminine; as the All-creative Mother; the consort of the Almighty Father, the Sun. According to many early myths, the human race was conceived in the womb of the Earth-Mother, and the first man and woman came forth from the under-world. To this day we talk of men as creatures of earth; as coming from the earth and returning to the earth, and in our burial custom we are but continuing the ancient practice, that had its origin with prehistoric man, of reverentially giving back to Mother Earth the children of her womb.

When once the idea became general that our world is feminine, it was but reasonable that natural orifices should have been regarded as typical of that part which characterizes woman, and this religious regard for openings in the earth naturally led to a like veneration for crevices or clefts in rocks, and finally for artificial openings or apertures, especially those connected with places of worship. In the vestibule of a church at Rome there is a large perforated stone, in the hole of which the Romans are said to have placed their hands while swearing a solemn oath ; a practice analogous to that of the Hebrews.

As at birth, a new being issues from the mother, so it was supposed that emergence from a terrestial or other sanctified cleft was equivalent to a new birth—to regeneration, —and in many places it was a common practice for parents to sanctify their children by passing them through openings and crevices.

Artificial holes, designed for purposes of purification, are still to be seen in some of the ancient religious structures of the British Isles and India ; the stones in a certain part of the building being so arranged as to have a hole under them, through which the devotees passed, and were thus purified or " born again."

Similar customs are still practised in parts of India. On the Island of Bombay, at Malabar Hill, there is a rock, upon the surface of which is a natural crevice, which connects with a cavity opening below. This is used by the Gentoos as a means of purification, which they say is effected by going in at the lower opening and emerging from the cavity above. A similar practice is more extensively observed in the northern portion of India, where there is a celebrated place to which many pilgrims go, to pass through an opening in the mountain; the performance being known as "passing through the Cow's Belly." In other places this mode of purification is accomplished by passing through an artificial structure in the shape of a cow; the devotees going in at the mouth and emerging at the rear.

The cow has always been regarded as a particularly holy emblem of the feminine deity. As the incarnation of Isis it was worshiped by the Egyptians with a veneration equal to that bestowed upon the bull. Many of the ancient temples dedicated to the feminine deity contained golden images of the cow or calf, and we are all familiar with the adoration paid by the Israelites to this creature as a sacred symbol. "And when the people saw that Moses delayed to come down out of the mount, the people gathered themselves together unto Aaron, and said unto him, Up, make us gods which shall go before us ;" and when the image of the calf had been made from the golden earrings of the people, it was worshiped with loud rejoicings as the representative of the deity that was to lead them out of the wilderness.

In later years Rehoboam, the king of the Israelites, likewise made two calves of gold, and said unto the people, "Behold thy gods, O Israel, which brought thee up out of the land of Egypt ;" clearly demonstrating that the cow or calf was persistently regarded as a sacred symbol, notwithstanding that the worship of such images was forbidden by the Mosaic law.

A symbol of equal significance with that of the opening or aperture, but of far greater sanctity and importance, was the chest or ark, or any consecrated repository or enclosure. The yoni was the receptacle, the divine ark, of the phallus ; within its hidden enclosure was contained the mystery of life. Its interior, to which the phallus, the Creator, alone had access, was the holy of holies. This was symbolized by the ark, the holiest of all symbols in the worship and ceremonies of the ancients. The most sacred object connected with the worship of Osiris was the ark, containing the divine symbol of life.

The Jewish ark of the covenant, which in size and manner of construction very closely resembled the sacred ark of the Egyptians, was the most important and holy feature in the life and worship of the Israelites. It was always guarded with the greatest care and veneration by the priests, and when moved from one place to another, was borne upon the shoulders of the Levites and attended with a grand ceremonial procession, " with shouting and with sound of the cornet and with trumpets and with cymbals, making a noise with psalteries and harps."

The ark was the divine symbol of the earth, of the female principle, containing the germ of all animated nature, and regarded as the Great Mother from whom all things come. It was likewise the symbol of salvation ; the place of safety, the sacred receptacle of the divine wisdom and power ; hence, the ark of the covenant was the holy abiding place of the tables of law that had been handed to Moses by the Lord. It also contained Aaron's rod, which sprang into life and budded, conveying the idea of symbolized fertility, and thus making the ark the repository of the emblem of the creative deity. To this day the ark is retained as a religious symbol in the Christian church; for the Roman Catholic pyx, the holy receptacle of the body of Christ, is but an adaptation of the ark, and has the same purpose and significance as the ancient symbol.

The ark of the Egyptians contained the symbols of the Triune Creator; the phallus, the egg and the serpent; the first representing the Sun, the male generative principle, the active Creator; the second, the Preserver; the passive, female principle; and the third, the Destroyer, or Reproducer. The egg as an emblem of the female principle was a very common emblem in all ancient faiths. It was considered as containing the germ of all life; the image of that which produced all things in itself; the emblem of life regenerated. As a symbol of the reproduction or resurrection of life it is still employed in the modern Easter celebration, as it was in similar celebrations in all past ages.

The moon, like the earth, being receptive only, was in a similar manner regarded as feminine, and was not infrequently worshiped as an actual deity—the Lunar Goddess. Ever remaining the same from year to year, unchanged by age and unweakened by use, the ancients came to think of the moon as the ever-continuing virgin wife of the sun, and the virgin mother of all inferior deities. This naturally led to the adoption of representations of the moon as peculiarly significant symbols of the feminine principle of nature, the chief of these being the crescent as an emblem of virginity. This is one of the most common and widely diffused feminine emblems, and to the present day amulets in the shape of a crescent are worn by the women of Italy and are regarded as especially appropriate to virgins and pregnant women.

In pictorial representations of the yoni, as the symbol of the feminine procreative power, it is often portrayed with more realism than is to be found in its images. This is especially true when shown in its place on the female form, as is common on ancient coins, vases, sculptures and in designs on temples. Women with exaggerated pudenda are frequently depicted on sacred lamps and other church utensils, and until within a short time ago several churches in Ireland had over their main entrance an elaborate sculpture of a woman pointing to her yoni. A similar design was to be seen on the side of a church entrance at Servatos, in Spain, while an equally phallic man was exhibited on the opposite side.

Symbolical designs of a similar character are still to be seen in India, plainly inscribed on the temples or carved in stone and placed on the walls. Over the gates of one of the cities of the ancient province of Sirinpatau stands a life-size stone statue of Sita, one of the feminine deities of procreation, while on each side of her are three naked penitents on their knees, engaged in the act prescribed by the ancient ritual for the adoration of this goddess.

In many cases, especially in the ancient

temples of Mexico, Yucatan and Peru, the keystone over the portal was adorned with a picture or carving of the yoni. Our modern use of the horsehoe as an emblem of good luck owes its origin to this custom of placing a design of the yoni above the door as a talisman; the horseshoe being adopted because of its resemblance to the form which the representation of the yoni most frequently assumed.

The pointed oval was one of the most common of the more conventional designs of the yoni, and in various modifications is still retained in our church architecture, as may be seen in the shape of the doors, the windows and arches. This symbolical oval was frequently referred to as the "Door of Life," and is to be seen in its true yonic significance in many ancient as well as modern religious designs. Virgin mothers and feminine deities were generally represented standing within a frame of this shape, and there are still in existence medals that were worn by Christian pilgrims to the shrine of the Virgin of Amadon, on which is inscribed a design of this character, which was commonly known as "The Mother and Child in the Door of Life."

As was pointed out in the case of the phallus, so it may be shown that many natural objects were chosen as emblems of the yoni, because of some resemblance to that symbol. Among the most common and familiar emblems of this character is the conch shell, which is still worn as an amulet in various parts of the world, as it was by the devout women of antiquity.

The fish, too, is a well-known religious symbol, sacred originally to Ishtar, Venus and other feminine deifications of the sexual nature. This was chosen partly on account of its fecundity and partly because its mouth was supposed to resemble the opening into the womb. Piscatorial designs are frequently met with on ancient temples and coins and are not uncommon in the present-day symbology of India, one of the principle designs being that of Vishnu emerging from the mouth of a great fish. The bishop's mitre is a modified form of a fish's head and mouth ; a style of religious head-dress that resulted from the ancient practice of the priests of Nineveh, whose veneration for the fish as a holy emblem led them to adopt a form of dress resembling as far as possible the outward appearance of this sacred creature.

The fish was a common symbol of Freya, the Scandinavian Venus, from whom is derived the name of the sixth day of the week, as on that day the Scandinavians honored their goddess of love by offerings of her sacred emblem; a custom which we still observe by eating fish on Friday.

In this connection it might be of interest to call attention to the fact, that three prominent phallic emblems have been retained by us as designs for weather vanes— the fish, the cock and the arrow. These emblems originally surmounted the towers and spires of religious buildings, but since their primitive significance has become obsolete, they have been relegated to the barns and stables.

The fig tree is a particularly appropriate and suggestive emblem in sex worship. Its trilobed leaf is emblematical of the masculine triad, and was commonly used and referred to in that sense, and hence its use as a symbolical covering for the private parts of a nude figure. Besides its masculine suggestiveness, this tree had also a feminine significance, from the fact that its fruit was supposed to bear a strong likeness to the shape of the virgin uterus, and that the eating of it was thought to promote fecundity.

It is evident, therefore, that this tree was one of unusual sacredness and significance, and in the early religious records is frequently used as a figure of speech for the expression of sentiments and ideas, which are unintelligible to those unacquainted with the many symbolical meanings that have been ascribed to this important tree. "To sit under the vine and fig tree;" "Don't care a fig," and other like expressions, are all of sexual significance.

In addition to the fig, a great many other trees and fruits were symbolical of the procreative functions; as the pomegranate, the fir, the apple, the cedar, the palm, grapes, vines and berries; all of which, together with several other examples, are alluded to in their figurative sense in the Song of Solomon. This song represents an amatory duet between Solomon and the daughter of Pharaoh on the occasion of their nuptials, and is supposed to be but one of a thousand similar love-songs and odes composed by king Solomon. This particular composition is regarded as the song of songs, and is, indeed, an exquisite poem, being preserved among the books of the Bible as emblematical of the love between Christ and the Church.

This song affords a striking example of what has been said regarding the purity of sexuality, when made the object of or connected with religious veneration. Hundreds of thousands of modest and devout men and women reverently read the Song of Solomon and fail to see in its amatory language anything but what is pure and holy ; and yet were this song to be read by one who understood not its religious significance, it could not but impress him as highly erotic and sensual. When the lover, speaking to his beloved one, says, "Thy thighs are like jewels ; thy navel is like a round goblet ; thy belly is like an heap of wheat set about with lilies," the reverent Christian sees only a poetic description of the Church. And when, in turn, the woman says of the man, " His cheeks are as a bed of spices ; his lips like lilies, his belly as bright ivory, and his legs as pillars of marble, set upon sockets of fine gold," and " he shall lie all night betwixt my breasts," the pious reader beholds naught but a holy figurative expression of the love of the Church for the Saviour.

With this Song in mind, let us not hastily condemn those who formerly indulged in similar or other forms of sexual expressions of religion, however gross or sensual they may appear to us in our ignorance of the religious meaning attached to them.

CHAPTER VIII.

THE SERPENT AND THE CROSS.

Serpent worship, next to the adoration of the phallus, is one of the most remarkable and at the same time one of the most widespread and persistent forms of religion the world has ever known. There is not a country of the ancient world, in the western as well as the eastern hemisphere, where it cannot be traced, pervading every known faith and system of theology, and leaving abundant proofs of its existence and extent, in the shape of monuments, temples and earthworks, as well as in designs and inscriptions.

No other symbol has been invested with such a variety of meanings and uses as has that of the serpent. It typified Wisdom, Power, Eternity, Good, Evil, Life, Reproduction and various other attributes of the creative principle. It entered into the mythology of every nation—Egypt, Syria, Greece, India, China, Scandinavia, America ; in short, there was no portion of the globe in which it was not recognized. It consecrated almost every temple, it symbolized almost every deity, it was imagined in the heavens, stamped on the earth, and ruled in the realms of everlasting sorrow.

That the serpent was a phallic symbol there is no doubt, for its worship is coeval with that of the phallus and formed part of the religion of every sex-worshiping nation, and while the meanings attached to it were numerous and various, they all had reference to the creative or reproductive principle of nature, and are readily reducible to the fundamental worship of procreation.

In many instances the serpent was employed as a symbol of the Creator, of the masculine element of generation, because of its shape and mobility ; a living phallus, as it were, actuated by its self-animating spirit, moving without hands or feet or any of the external members by which other beings effect their motion. Among most of the eastern nations, however, it had a more subtle significance, in that it represented an emotion or a feeling rather than a material object or actuality. While in a general sense it typified the Creator, its specific office was the symbolization of the animating spirit of procreation, the stimulating factor in the production and immortality of life.

This potent, energizing factor was the sexual instinct, the Divine Passion. In it the ancient philosophers beheld the vital source of procreation, the moving energy in the production of life and the population of the world; and hence to them this divine passion, this all-pervading, impelling force, was the actuating, creative spirit of the Almighty. Consequently, it became an object of veneration as the divine spiritual agent in the great mystery of life, and, naturally, its worshipers sought for it some suggestive symbol, with the result that the serpent was chosen, as most fully and comprehensively embodying the various attributes of the Creator in his subtle and omnipotent power.

In all probability, the cobra de capello, or hooded snake of India, was the particular species of the reptile first adopted as an emblem of the Divine Passion, because of its highly suggestive peculiarities. It has the power of puffing itself up, enlarging and erecting its head, when aroused to excitement, and its size, shape, position, and regular pulsations when in this condition, as well as its well-known power of fascination, were all extremely significant, and readily appealed to the fancy and superstition of an emotional and religious race.

All of the more ancient representations of the serpent in the symbology of Egypt, Babylon, Persia, Greece, and other countries bear a strong resemblance to the cobra; but after the adoption of this species as a religious emblem it was not long before the significance attached to this particular kind was extended to the serpent in general, and hence we find that each nation had its own particular variety of snake as a sacred symbol of the Divine Passion, or invigorating energy of nature, in its various interpretations of Wisdom, Eternity, Life, Reproduction, and so on.

The important significance of the serpent is shown by the fact that this animal was employed in all the phallic rites and ceremonies of the ancients, and was an object of worship to every nation on the globe. According to the Bible, the brazen serpent made by Moses at the command of the Lord was regarded with the deepest veneration by the Israelites, and was religiously preserved and worshiped by them for a period of seven hundred years, when it was finally destroyed by Hezekiah, because of the idolatrous rites connected with its worship.

All celebrations, especially those in honor of the procreative deities, were attended with the exhibition and adoration of the serpent. In the mysteries of Egypt, Greece and Rome, the sacred reptile was carried in the processions by troops of noble virgins, and many of the people had living snakes entwined about their heads, or carried them in their hands, while shouting with religious excitement. Nearly every ancient city of the East, as well as in Mexico and other portions of America, had its serpent temple, in which were kept enormous specimens of this sacred reptile, that were worshiped and waited upon with divine honors.

Though as a general rule, the serpent was venerated and adored as the representative of divine power, wisdom and goodness, it was also not infrequently employed as the symbol of evil. This naturally resulted from its use as an emblem of the sexual desire, for while this instinct was on the one hand recognized and worshiped as the divine factor in the work of the Creator, and hence the source of all good, it was equally the source of all evil. It was through it that sin came into the world; it was the blind, overmastering passion that incited mankind to disobedience and wickedness; the inflaming spirit of lust; the tempter, and the seducer. Consequently, the serpent became the representative of sin, the personification of evil; and this devil, this opposer of God, or the Good, was the sexual nature, in its sensual and lustful aspect.

Accordingly, it is not difficult to comprehend the allegorical significance of the serpent in the account of the temptation and

THE SERPENT AND THE CROSS. 129

fall of Adam and Eve. Their sin consisted in acquainting themselves with fleshly enjoyments. They resisted not the promptings of their sexual desires, but permitted themselves to partake of the forbidden fruit.

The symbolism of the serpent is very extensive and is met with in a great variety of forms and combinations. It is, however, seldom found as an isolated symbol, except in the well-known Egyptian design, in which it is shown with its tail in its mouth, as an emblem of immortality and future life. As a rule, it appears in conjunction with male or female emblems, and one of the oldest and best-known phallic representations in which the serpent figures, is the Rod of Life, or the caduceus of Mercury.

This represents two serpents twined about an upright staff or pole, and typifies the phallus receiving life and potency from the Divine Energy. Its special significance is due to the position of the serpents, which is that adopted by the cobra when mating. A Hindoo regards it as a most fortunate omen to be able to witness this serpentine union, and it is said that if while in this condition a cloth be thrown over the serpents it becomes endowed with extraordinary powers. Pieces of cloth that have been thus encharmed are preserved with the greatest care and veneration as talismans for averting evil influences or for securing conjugal blessings.

The staff of life in a great variety of forms is common on ancient coins, gems, and sculptures. In many designs the serpent is shown in conjunction with both male and female symbols, and ever has for its significance the Divine Passion, the invigorating and inspiring energy of nature.

This divine, actuating force of nature owed its sacredness to the fact that it was the necessary and inciting means to the accomplishment of the supreme life-purpose of man and woman—the union of the two for the reproduction of life and the perpetuation of the race. It was in the gratification of the Divine Passion that man experienced his most exalted pleasure, and beheld the direct and immediate cause of a new being and the immortality of life. Hence, the act of generation, the union of the sexes, was regarded as supremely sacred and divine. It was the sublime means ordained by the Creator for the fulfillment of his infinite purpose ; and, as will be more fully shown in a subsequent chapter, was regarded as a most holy act and was the object of universal worship and of devout, religious rites.

Many realistic figures and designs were employed to represent this holy union of the sexes, and may still be seen on the temples and monuments of ancient Egypt and of India. The most extensive and sacred symbol of the Hindoos is the lingam-in-yoni, an image made of wood or stone, in representation of the union of the lingam and yoni.

Symbols of like significance, in endless varieties of design and size, were common among the ancients, but pre-eminent among them all was the cross, which, in its original and primitive form, was merely a simplification of the various designs used to represent the congress of the sexes. These in their general outline and shape consisted of an upright portion, connected at right angles with a horizontal base; the whole resembling, to a greater or less extent, an inverted T (⊥); and this simplified form, when made of stone or wood and set up on end, in order to be more plainly exhibited, resulted in the figure of the cross.

From time immemorial the cross has been used as a religious symbol. There is no portion of the world inhabited by man in which it is not found, and there is no time in the history of the world—back even to the ages of the prehistoric man,—that this sacred symbol has not been in existence. It was universally regarded as the emblem of life, of regeneration, or of immortality, and was ever held in the highest veneration as the holiest of all symbols.

It appears in a great variety of shapes; all of which, however, are readily reducible to the simple, primary form. The cross of four arms meeting at right angles, and commonly called the Greek cross, is found on Assyrian tablets, on Egyptian and Persian monuments and on Etruscan jars and vases; while the Latin cross, the one now used as a Christian symbol, is to be seen on equally ancient coins, monuments and pottery, and stone images of it have been found in the remains of temples and habitations that existed hundreds and even thousands of years before the time of Christ.

A modified form of this cross is the *crux ansanta*, or handled cross, so called because the part above the cross-beam is in the form of an oval loop, and served as a handle for holding the image. This cross is found in most of the religious scenes pictured on the temples of ancient Egypt, and is most commonly shown in the hands of Isis, Osiris and other divinities, while images of it are not infrequently found on the breasts of mummies. Assyrian and Babylonian sculptures frequently exhibit this form of the cross, and it is prominently shown on some of the coins found in the temple of Serapis.

Early Phenician coins bear the design of a semi-circular chain of beads with the cross attached; similar in every respect to the modern rosary. Rosaries of the same kind are also found among the Buddhists of Japan and the Lamas of Thibet.

In the cave of Elephanta, near Bombay, is a sculpturing that records the destruction of the male children at the birth of Krishna, the Hindoo saviour, who lived about fifteen hundred years before Christ, and over the head of the executioner, who is surrounded with supplicating mothers, is a cross.

When the Spaniards came to America they were astonished to find that the natives of Mexico not only had the cross as a religious symbol, but that they worshiped a crucified saviour and a virgin mother. These unaccountable features of their religion led to the invention by the Christians of a legend, that St. Thomas had miraculously come over to America centuries before and had revealed the doctrines of the church to the Mexicans. But this legend would fail to account for the existence of the cross and other Christian symbols found in the remains of the prehistoric races of Central America.

In the midst of the forests of Yucatan is a ruined city. It had long been dead and overgrown at the time of the conquest of Mexico. According to tradition, it was founded nine hundred years before Christ. In this ancient city of Palenque was found a building of religious worship, containing several altars, and at the back of one of them was discovered a stone slab, on which were sculptured two human figures standing one on each side of a cross, to which one of the figures was extending his arms and offering an infant.

The earliest and most primitive form of the cross was one in the shape of the letter **T**, commonly called the *tau* cross. This was the old Scandinavian symbol of the god Thor, and is found among the very oldest nations of the world. It was the mark that the Israelites put on their doorposts with the blood of the lamb, on the occasion of the Passover, and in the book of Ezekiel we read that this same sacred and talismanic sign was directed by the Lord to be placed on the foreheads of the men of Jerusalem who were to be spared in the destruction of the city : " Slay utterly old and young, both maids and little children and women ; but come not near any man upon whom is the mark." Images of this shape were commonly used in the religious rites of the ancients, and it was customary among some of the eastern races for the women to sacrifice their virginity by rupturing the hymen with a small stone or iron cross of this kind.

For three or four centuries after Christ the *tau* cross was employed almost exclusively by the followers of the new religion, and inscriptions of it, as well as of the *crux ansanta*, may be seen on the early tombs and monuments of the Christians. At first, however, the use of the cross in any form was not permitted by the church fathers, because it was a pagan symbol, and its introduction into Christian celebrations was sternly forbidden as rank profanation.

Though it is popularly believed that our familiar church symbol represents the form of the cross on which Christ was crucified, there is absolutely no authority for this belief, as there is in existence no authentic record describing the form of the cross on which Jesus was executed. These instruments of execution were of various shapes; the simplest form being an upright stake, on which the malefactor was sometimes impaled, and sometimes fastened with cords or nails. In the other forms, the transverse beam was frequently separate from the upright, and this was the only part borne by the victim to the place of execution. Christ, therefore, was not obliged to carry the entire cross, as is generally supposed, and represented in pictures, but simply the crosspiece, which was fastened to the upright stake after he reached Calvary.

From the fact that the early Christians used the *tau* cross as a symbol of the crucifixion, it is probable that that was the form of cross on which Christ met his death, and this is the opinion held by most scholars and investigators.

Through all the ages of humankind, the cross has been the dearest and holiest of emblems, and to the devout worshiper of to-day it is the same glorious symbol of redemption and resurrection that it was to the man or woman of five thousand years ago. Primarily representing the divine union of the sexes, it has ever typified regeneration and the life everlasting.

CHAPTER IX.

THE DIVINE ACT.

The universal employment of the cross in all ages as a symbol of life and immortality demonstrates most conclusively the innate and overmastering reverence of mankind for the divine act of generation,—the union of the sexes,—not only because of the ecstatic exaltation that it inspired (which, in many of the ancient religious and philosophical writings, is regarded as a momentary union with God, an absorption into the Divine Soul), but because of its wonderful and sublime result. It was the acme of human bliss, a glimpse of the Divine Nature, the immortalizing act of God. It was this which first awoke in man a realization of the soul, a belief in the immortality of life.

To the philosophers of antiquity man and woman in their individualities were incomplete creatures; they were but component parts of one being. They had in them the potentiality of reproduction and immortality, but in themselves they were barren and impotent. It was only in their union, in their reciprocal and co-operative activity, that they became one,—a perfect soul. Only then were they capable of fulfilling the divine will for which they were mutually created.

It is by no means surprising, therefore, that this wondrous and omnipotent act should have been made the object of divine worship, and to this day the union of the sexes is solemnized with religious ceremonies, in continued recognition of its holiness. According to law, marriage is simply a civil contract, a mere agreement to live together, and may be executed before any duly qualified officer of the law; but the vast majority of us prefer that this contract should be made the occasion of a religious celebration. In fact, many believe that marriage is not valid unless performed by a representative of the Lord and attended with blessings and ceremonial rites. The nuptial tie is held to be a divine bond,—

"Those whom God hath joined together let no man put asunder."

And, after all, what is the object of a marriage ceremony but a sanctification of the sexual union? Reverence for the sacredness of this union is still inherent in mankind, and, because of its holiness, cannot be consummated until properly sanctioned and hallowed by these religious ceremonies. To engage in the act of generation in the absence of such consecratory rites, is regarded as a wrong or a crime, even as it was four and five thousand years ago.

In all ancient religions this reverent regard for the divine act of creation led to the adoption of various rites and practices for the sanctification of sexual unions, not only in the form of marriage, but of prostitution, which, under certain circumstances, was considered both proper and holy. Every ancient temple had connected with it a number of consecrated women, whose office it was to submit themselves to the embraces of any man who might come in unto them, upon the payment of a specified sum; the money thus received being used for religious purposes.

To the minds of the ancients no more appropriate nor holy means could be devised for raising money for the maintenance of the temple than a sanctified indulgence in the Divine Act. It was the most sublime and sacred of all human functions —the consummation of God's will,—and consequently God's temple was the most fitting place for its performance.

One of the earliest allusions to these consecrated temple-women is found in the book of Genesis, where we are told that Tamar deceived her father-in-law, Judah, by veiling herself after the manner of the women of the temple, and sitting before the door of Enajim, where Judah beheld her and went in unto her. The women of this class wore a special attire, the principal feature of which was a long veil, and conducted themselves quietly, not seeking customers, but waiting for them to make the first approach. In this guise Tamar succeeded in enticing Judah, who thought she was a temple attendant and, consequently, one with whom he was permitted to associate. The ordinary harlot of the Hebrews was an outcast, and was conspicuous by her immodest attire and bold conduct, it being not unusual for women of this character to rush up to men and kiss them in public.

Consecrated prostitution was common among all the early nations of the world, and was everywhere regarded in the most sacred light. Some of the ancient places of worship were devoted entirely to this holy purpose, as appears from the fact that the chief temple of Babylon was called Bit-Shaggathu, which means, literally, the Temple for Copulation.

The number of women attached to some of these places was very large; the temple of Venus at Corinth having no less than a thousand sacred prostitutes connected with it, while a similar number belonged to the temple of the same goddess at Eryx. In later times, among the Greeks and Romans, this practice lost much of its religious aspect, degenerating into sheer licentiousness, and Juvenal tells us that every temple in Rome was practically a licensed brothel.

This practice, in its religious purity, is still in vogue in many parts of India, where every important temple belonging to the worshipers of what is known as the Sacteyan faith has attached to it a troop of nautch girls, or "women of the idol," who are considered as holy devotees of the faith. These girls are chosen by the priests, when quite young, on account of their beauty, health and activity, and it is regarded as a rare honor by parents to have a daughter selected for this holy profession; even high officials and dignitaries looking upon it as a proud distinction.

Among some of the Hindoo sects these consecrated girls are considered particularly sacred, as personifications of the goddess Bhagavatee, and are the objects of devout adoration. Many persons perform the worship of these girls daily. This is done by placing the girl, generally in a nude condition, upon a seat with flowers, paints, scented water and fruits, and addressing to her prayers and expressions of adoration. She is then presented with costly offerings of cloth, ornaments and wines, and at the conclusion of the ceremony, which is a lengthy and elaborate one, the worshiper offers incense and prostrates himself before the living idol.

After reaching sexual maturity these girls are initiated into the mysteries and duties of their profession by the consummation of their marriage to the god. Their great natural beauty is heightened by all the enticements of drapery, jewels, seductive arts and general feminine witchery. Of all their arts dancing is the most highly cultivated; not, however, the mode of dancing to which we are accustomed, but consisting of a pantomime made up of the most graceful and alluring dramatic action, gestures, twistings and marvelous undulatory and expressive motions of the arms and legs and the whole body; a performance which is at once poetical, sensual and skillful, and constitutes the chief ostensible employment of these nautch girls.

Their true office, however, is to secure revenue for the sustenance and enrichment of the temple by giving themselves to all who desire and are willing to pay for their possession. As they are beautiful, and accomplished in all seductive and passion-alluring arts, and are safe companions by reason of their perfect state of health, and as it is considered both honorable and holy on their part, as well as on the part of their patrons, thus to swell the treasury of the temple, it need not be wondered at that they are much sought after and well paid for this part of their services.

These consecrated women are treated with the greatest reverence and respect; while a Hindoo woman who prostitutes herself for private gain, is an outcast and bears a disgraceful name; a further illustration of the sanctity attached to the Divine Act and of the pollution and profanation resulting from its performance in the absence of religious auspices.

Among many of the ancients it was taught that sexual indulgence was the true and only aim in life and that it was a religious duty every man and woman owed to

God, the Creator. This doctrine was not infrequently carried to its extreme; nor was it peculiar alone to the people of antiquity, for we find that in the Middle Ages certain sects of Christians held that true blessedness on earth consisted in the full and unstinted enjoyment of venereal pleasures, which were ordained by the Lord as the divine means of fulfilling his glorious purpose and of bringing mankind more closely into communion with himself and with the eternal blessedness that awaited them hereafter. This idea was in some instances carried to such an extent, that not only were gross sensuality and crime permitted, but were actually recommended, if necessary for the attainment of the desired end.

According to one of these sects, the greatest of all sins (in fact, the only sin) consisted in opposing the appetites and passions. These were gifts of God; they were given to man for a divine purpose, and every inclination inspired by them must be fulfilled as a religious duty; a tenet which found many earnest followers, whose practices were fully in keeping with their beliefs. A custom adopted by them and religiously carried out, was that which required the host to offer his wife to any stranger or friend who was entertained at the house. To them genuine hospitality consisted in placing at the disposal of the visitor all that the host possessed, at the same time affording the guest an opportunity of indulging in the rite prescribed by the sect.

The custom in this case was noteworthy, because of its adoption and practice by civilized men; but it has always been a common feature of primitive social conditions, and at the present day it is to be found among many of the uncivilized people of the world. Among the coast tribes of British Columbia the present of a wife is one of the greatest honors that can be shown to a guest. The savage offers a visitor his wife as we offer him a seat at the table. It is not always the wife, however, that is offered; it is sometimes a daughter, a sister or a servant. Thus, the people of Madagascar warn strangers to behave with decency to their wives, while they readily and willingly offer their daughters. A Tungas will give his daughter for a time to any friend or traveler to whom he takes a fancy; and if he has no daughter, he will give a servant, but not his wife; while in other tribes wives are commonly given up and exchanged in token of friendship,— customs which will no doubt remind the reader of the practice in ancient Sparta of borrowing and loaning wives.

The worship of the act of generation was common to all nations of the world, and formed an important feature of many of their religious celebrations in honor of the procreative deities. Homage to the Creator consisted not only in offerings and songs of praise, but in the ceremonial exercise of the sacred function of generation itself; for, according to the teachings of all religions, no act can be more holy than that done in imitation of the Deity. To be as God, to do as he has done, to follow in his footsteps, are the golden and fundamental precepts of every religious faith. It was but natural, therefore, that the divine act of creation should have been devoutly performed as a religious rite, in the pious endeavor to thus imitate the Almighty in his glorious work of creation and reproduction, and that it should have been made the object of special worship.

A typical example of the manner in which this ancient rite was frequently performed is to be found at this day among the Kauchiluas of India. This has been described by a writer as "a peculiar rite that throws into confusion all the ties of female relationship." Social restraints are wholly obliterated for the time being, in honor of the Creator and his divine function. The women—maids and matrons—deposit their bodices in a box, each garment and each woman being numbered by a priest. At the close of the ritual of song and prayer, each male worshiper takes a bodice from the box, and the woman who has the number corresponding to that on the garment, even though it be the sister or daughter of the man who draws it, becomes his partner for the fulfillment of that which has been the subject of their worship and praise during the preceding ceremonies.

This rite and the wild excesses that are sometimes incidental to it are engaged in by the most devout and pure-minded men and women, the majority of whom, outside of this ceremony (which they consider a sacred and solemn observance of their faith), are as modest and chaste as any devotees of their more enlightened fellow-beings of the western world.

Indiscriminate intercourse of this kind was indulged in in the temples, as a customary feature of the vernal festivals of the Greeks and Romans, held in honor of the procreative deities, and was condoned and recommended as a proper and appropriate means of glorifying the gods.

Festivals of a similar kind were celebrated throughout Egypt, in honor of Isis and Osiris, the deities of procreation. The celebration at Mendes was particularly noteworthy, for it was there that the sacred goat was employed in the ceremonies. These were of an intensely religious character, inducing a high state of excitement and enthusiasm, at the climax of which many of the women offered themselves to the goat as the divine representative of the Deity.

We are told by Herodotus that the goat accepted this unnatural copulation and that the union took place publicly in the assembly, being regarded by all as a most holy and sacred performance; and the women who thus gave their persons were held in particular reverence thereafter as the recipients of divine favor. This particular feature of the celebration was not, however, confined to the women, as is shown by frequent references in ancient records and by Egyptian sculptures representing the union of men and female goats.

As was stated before, such rites were performed through a truly devout and religious desire to honor the Deity and win his favor, by imitating the divine act by which life is regenerated and immortalized. Among some of the ancient peoples, this divine generative function was typified by the public union of a man and woman; a performance which was attended with elaborate religious ceremonies and constituted the most sacred and holy feature of their worship. This particular rite is still practised by some of the phallic-worshiping sects of India, and is to be met with among the natives of some of the Pacific islands. A navigator, writing of one of their religious festivals, says: "A young man of fine size and perfect proportions performed the creative act with a little miss of eleven or twelve before the assembled congregation, among whom were the leading people of rank of both sexes, without any thought of observing otherwise than an appropriate religious duty."

Accounts of many other ceremonies celebrated in honor of the divine procreative function, might be given, but those already cited are sufficient to demonstrate how general and how persistent through all time has been man's reverence for the immortalizing act of generation, and that in every age and in every country mankind has endeavored to honor and glorify the Author of Life by appropriate religious ceremonies.

CHAPTER X.

REGENERATION.

In all mythologies and religious creeds the regeneration of life figures as a prominent and fundamental feature. Clothed in a countless variety of myths, beliefs and doctrines, this glorious phase of nature and of life has from time immemorial been the object of man's joyous worship, as a typification of immortality and of the redemption of mankind. Through all ages the nations of the world have celebrated the renewal of life with gladsome religious festivals ; festivals that, in various modifications, are retained to this day, and form the chief and most glorious feature of modern religious worship.

There is not a time in the history of the human race of which we have any record, that mankind did not celebrate the vernal reanimation of nature ; the resurrection of life. It was in the spring that the world, the Earth Mother, was quickened by the vitalizing power of the sun, the Creator. Life was re-born. The earth once more awoke with renewed vitality and beauty. All the world, all nature was a triumphant symbolization of life's regeneration, and hence the springtime became the chosen season for joyous festivals, in honor of the Creator and his wondrous powers.

After a glorious reign in the heavens, beneath which the earth revels in joyousness and beauty, the sun enters the wintry realms of the southern sky, leaving the world cold and cheerless; and after an absence of several months, during which all nature mourns and weeps, he reappears in the gloriousness of his light and potency, and brings back to earth the life and the joy that have lain dead and cold beneath the ban of winter. To primitive man these seasonal events were of the most vital import. To him they meant more than mere natural phenomena. They were the supreme manifestations of the universal life in its wondrous phases of birth, death and resurrection. Spring, summer, autumn, winter, the months, the earth, the sun and the multitude of features and phenomena incident to the annual revolution of the earth became living entities, personifications of beings and deities, whose relationship one to the other, and the parts they played in the great drama of nature, gave rise to those myths and legends that, as before stated, constitute the basis of every system of mythology and every theological creed.

In many instances the sun, or life, in its garb of summer, was personified as a youth, who, like Baldur, the Scandinavian summer-god, is slain through the treachery of the evil being representing the frost or the chilling month of December, and is carried to the under-world, there to remain as a captive of the god of winter, but eventually to return to earth and once more gladden it with his presence. Again, as in the myth connected with the Eleusinian mysteries of the Greeks, life is a maiden—Persephone,—who is carried away by Pluto to the realm of shades, but through the supplications of her mother, Demeter, the goddess of the earth, she is permitted to return to the world every summer.

From such simple myths there arose legends and beliefs of a more elaborate and theological character. The sun in his annual journey became the almighty Creator himself, in the form of a divine Saviour, glorifying the world with his potent and sublime presence, and meeting his death through the betrayal of one of his attendants (the personifications of the months or the twelve signs of the zodiac); only to rise again, however, in all his glory and supremacy of power, for the salvation of man.

This version we find represented in the legend of Osiris, the Creator and Saviour of the Egyptians, and in a more elaborate form it appears in the story of Krishna, the Hindoo Saviour and Son of God, who was born of a virgin, about four thousand years ago. His advent was heralded by the joyful pæans of angels, who appeared in the heavens at night and announced the glad tidings to the wondering and awe-struck mortals. Upon the announcement of his birth the governor of the province in which he was born ordered the killing of all the male infants, out of fear for this newborn ruler; yet the Saviour miraculously escaped. Accompanied by his disciples, to whom he was known as Jezeus, he traveled about the country, working miracles and preaching the gospel of peace, until he was finally executed and suspended on the branches of a tree, from which he miraculously disappeared, to return to earth for the final redemption of mankind.

The ancient springtime festivals, celebrated in honor of the resurrected life, reached their highest and most elaborate development in Egypt, Greece and Rome, and were commonly known as the "mysteries." These mysteries constituted the most important and sacred feature of ancient religious worship, and have left their impress on every age and generation, down to the present day, in the shape of mystic orders and secret societies.

They were so called because of the secrecy in which many of their rites were conducted, and because of the deep and holy mystery attached to them. This love of the mysterious is inherent in the human race and, as may be imagined, was exhibited in its most intense form among the emotional and superstitious people of antiquity.

The symbols and rites of their celebrations were invested by the priests with a mystical and occult significance, unintelligible to the masses and confided only to those who, after most severe trials of faith and endurance, were found worthy of initiation into the divine secrets. They were then made acquainted with the exalted and abstruse doctrines evolved by the priesthood from the simple worship of nature; doctrines that constituted a theosophy of the most transcendent and spiritual character; grand and sublime in the loftiness of its teachings and ideality and in the beauty of its poetic conceptions.

The mysteries of Isis and Osiris, of Egypt, the mysteries of the Babylonians, the Eleusinian mysteries of the Greeks, the mysteries of Bacchus and Venus at Rome, together with many others of lesser importance, were all festivals in celebration of the new-born life and the regenerative union of the creative elements of nature. They all set forth and illustrated by solemn and impressive rites and mystical symbols the grand phenomena of nature in its creation and perpetuation of life.

Among the Greeks and Romans these vernal festivals were held in honor of Bacchus, or Dionysos, the god of generative power, and his union with Persephone, the returned goddess of life. He was called the father of gods and men; "the Begotten of Love" (having been born of a virgin through immaculate love), and was frequently represented by the Romans under the name and form of Priapus.

Considering the general state of reserve and restraint in which the Grecian women lived, we may gain some idea of the high regard in which these observances were held, and the powerful influence they exercised over the mind and emotions, when we note to what a degree of extravagance the religious enthusiasm of these women was carried on such occasions, particularly at the celebration of the Eleusinian mysteries and the Bacchanalia. The gravest matrons and proudest princesses apparently laid aside all dignity and modesty, and vied with each other in revelry. They ran screaming through the woods and over mountains, fantastically dressed or half naked, their hair interwoven with ivy and vine leaves and not infrequently with living serpents, that twined about their heads and necks. Their religious excitement sometimes became so great that they ate raw flesh, tearing living animals to pieces with their teeth and devouring them while yet warm and palpitating.

On these festal occasions they likewise repaired to the temples or other places rendered sacred by the presence of the god's image, and there made offerings to the divine emblem by wreathing the phallus with flowers and anointing it with specially prepared wine. Their devotions were always accompanied with music and wine, which were considered the sacred means of exalting and raising the mind to a closer communion with the Divine Power; and these enthusiastic devotees willingly gave themselves up to the embraces of the no less enthusiastic worshipers of the opposite sex, in the nocturnal ceremonies, that had for their object the glorification of the deity by an indulgence in the divine act of generation.

The worship of the Greeks was quite as phallic as that of other nations, but their ceremonies were clothed in such attractive splendor, with a dramatic and poetic coloring so alluring and effective, and with a symbolism so beautiful and at the same time so comprehensively significant, and were conducted by an eloquent and cultured priesthood in accordance with a ritual so impressive and inspiring, so well calculated to arouse enthusiastic and heroic ardor, and so replete with charmingly sentimental, as well as subtly amorous suggestions, that the majority of the devotees became so exalted in their worship as to regard the sensual indulgences and erotic rites in which they engaged, as mere incidents rather than the true object of their springtime celebrations.

The Romans borrowed their religious

forms and rites from the Greeks, and while they did not imbibe the poetry, sentiment and enthusiasm that characterized the Grecian festivities, they were none the less devout and sincere. Their Bacchanalian mysteries were celebrated in the Temple of Bacchus at Rome and in the sacred woods near the Tiber. At first these ceremonies were held in the daytime and were attended only by the women, who were initiated into the mysteries by the priests; but they were subsequently celebrated at night and the initiation of young men was permitted, with the result that in a short time it led to the admittance of those who were not in sympathy with the religious spirit of the occasion, but took advantage of the opportunity for indulgence in licentious practices and other crimes, which were speedily confounded with the true object of the festival, and finally led to the abolishment of the celebration by a decree of the Senate.

The Liberalia, the Floralia, and the festival of Venus were popular vernal festivals celebrated by the Romans in honor of the procreative deities and their vitalizing function, as manifested by the glorious regeneration of life upon the earth. While these festivals were of a religious character, they were given up to mirth, jollity and public amusements, accompanied by a general relaxation of the laws and of social proprieties, as a fitting manner of celebrating the return of life and gladness.

These springtime festivals, in celebration of resurrected life and the generative powers of nature, were common among all nations from the earliest times, and it is in some of the particular forms of these celebrations that we find the origin of our own joyous festival—Easter. Among the old Teutons and Saxons the month of April was held sacred to Eastre, the Queen of Heaven, the Goddess of Life, and a feast of rejoicing was held in her honor at that time of the year. It was customary to make presents of eggs, which were brightly decorated or colored; the egg being the sacred emblem of the resurrection of life, and therefore used as an offering to the goddess on this occasion.

The early Germans and Franks also prepared a special kind of bread or bun, that was eaten at this time as especially sacred to Eastre.

Eggs and buns figured also in the Chaldean rites connected with the worship of the goddess of spring, the Renewer of Life, upwards of four thousand years ago, and were familiar features in the worship of the Queen of Heaven, Ishtar, as early as the days of Cecrops, the founder of Athens, fifteen hundred years before Christ.

These ancient buns, which were offered to the Queen of Heaven and used in sacrifices to other generative deities, were formed in the shape of the reproductive organs; a custom to which reference is made in the book of Jeremiah, where the prophet says, "The children gather wood, the fathers kindle the fire, and the women knead the dough to make cakes to the Queen of Heaven."

The practice of making Easter buns in this shape was common among some of the early Christians, and prevails in certain parts of France to this day. Small cakes in the shape of a phallus are made as offerings at Easter-time and carried about and presented from house to house. On the festival of Palm Sunday, sometimes known as the Feast of the Privy Members, it was customary, not long since in certain French provinces, for each of the women and children in the procession to carry a phallus, made of bread, attached to the end of a palm branch. These phalli were subsequently blessed by the priests and preserved by the women during the year.

The Egyptian mysteries were likewise a springtime celebration of the regeneration of life. These mysteries represented the death and resurrection of Osiris, the Creator and Saviour of men. The attendant ceremonies were of a most sacred and holy character, invested with the deepest mystery and sanctity. The sacred ark was reverently and tearfully worshiped as the sepulchre of the departed god, and the lamentations and mourning for his decease marked the beginning of the mysteries. On the third day of his death the priests, in solemn procession, proceeded to the river in the night, carrying the ark with them. Waiting there until the morning they welcomed the rising sun with a loud and joyous shout, exclaiming " Osiris is risen!"

It matters not to what race nor to what age we turn, we ever find the same reverent regard for the regeneration of life. Through all the myths and ceremonials of the world, however extravagant or inconsistent many of them may appear, we trace the constant aim of mankind to glorify the Creator and to honor him by the celebration of rites and festivals demonstrative of the adoration of mankind for his supreme powers, wisdom and goodness, while beneath them all lies the universal actuating reverence for the great and unsolvable mystery of procreation—the foundation of all religious worship.

www.ingramcontent.com/pod-product-compliance
Lightning Source LLC
Chambersburg PA
CBHW030251170426
43202CB00009B/707